SABOTAGE

SABOTAGE

AMERICA'S ENEMIES WITHIN THE CIA

ROWAN SCARBOROUGH

Since 1947
REGNERY
PUBLISHING, INC.

An Eagle Publishing Company • Washington, DC

Library of Congress Cataloging-in-Publication Data

Scarborough, Rowan.
  Sabotage : America's enemies within the CIA / Rowan Scarborough.
    p. cm.
  Includes index.
  ISBN 978-1-59698-510-0
  1. United States. Central Intelligence Agency. 2. Intelligence service—United States. 3. United States—Politics and government—2001– I. Title.
  JK468.I6S29 2007
  327.1273—dc22

                                    2007021233
  ISBN 978-1-59698-510-0

Published in the United States by
Regnery Publishing, Inc.
One Massachusetts Avenue, NW
Washington, DC 20001
www.regnery.com

Manufactured in the United States of America

10 9 8 7 6 5 4 3 2 1

Books are available in quantity for promotional or premium use. Write to Director of Special Sales, Regnery Publishing, Inc., One Massachusetts Avenue NW, Washington, DC 20001, for information on discounts and terms or call (202) 216-0600.

To my nephews, Chris Greer and Tim Greer,
who are serving their country

CONTENTS

A "ROGUE AGENCY"

Congressman Pete Hoekstra had seen and heard enough in the spring of 2006, when he dictated an extraordinary letter to President Bush. Hoekstra's private four-page message, printed on House Intelligence Committee letterhead, was a blunt warning to the nation's commander in chief. (See the Appendix.) An enemy lurked, the congressman said. Not Iran, North Korea, or al Qaeda and its legions of Islamic extremists. He wrote of an opponent right under the president's nose: the Central Intelligence Agency.

Hoekstra had heard privately from some of the president's national security advisors that they believed CIA factions were working against the president. Why, he wondered, didn't they do anything about it? "They know people within the CIA have been no help to their president," Hoekstra later told me. "I've stated to the president, 'You've got some people who may not necessarily be working for you.'"

The stakes were high that spring. Since the September 11, 2001, attacks on America, intelligence collection had become the number-one weapon in the attempt to defeat al Qaeda and Osama bin Laden. A plot penetrated is an attack stopped. To the outside observer, the CIA had performed well as a key partner in the Bush administration's War on Terror. The Agency's scorecard boasted the capture of Khalid Sheikh Mohammed, the architect of the September 11 attacks. He dished dirt under CIA pressure, enabling Washington and its allies to foil a number of planned attacks and murders. It was a great CIA coup. Republican Porter Goss, himself a former covert intelligence operative in Latin America who went on to represent Florida's Gulf Coast in Congress, had taken over at the CIA's helm two years earlier. The Agency's headquarters in the tony Langley neighborhood in Northern Virginia, run for more than ten years by Bill Clinton's choices, including holdover George Tenet, was now under complete GOP control. Or so it appeared.

There exists another storyline about the CIA, one with a far more unsettling plot, that reveals the true state of this crucial agency. The drama of this story is not the well-reported fact that the Agency committed two of the worst intelligence blunders of its history: failing to penetrate the September 11 plot (which was in the works for five years) and reporting to President Bush that Iraq was hiding huge quantities of chemical weapons and had reconstituted its nuclear weapons program when it had not.

The less-publicized story is this: Hoekstra's May 18, 2006, letter to President Bush warned that some within the analytical and operations branches had sabotaged the president and the War on Terror. "There has been much public and private speculation about the politicization of the agency," Hoekstra told Bush. "I am convinced that this politicization was under way well before Porter Goss became the director. In fact, I have been long concerned that a strong and well-positioned group within the agency intentionally undermined the administration and its policies." In a time of war, Bush faced an unprecedented challenge. An agency he relied on to fight terrorists was actually working against him, Hoekstra said.

What had happened? Since al Qaeda's murder of nearly three thousand people on September 11, Bush had been blindsided by a series of damaging leaks from "intelligence sources." Hoekstra, the intelligence committee chairman, claimed these leaks came from Langley itself. White House aides complained among themselves that they were fighting three enemies: al Qaeda, the Democrats, and the CIA. And amid one of the frequent battles of words between the White House and unnamed CIA officials, Senate Intelligence Committee chairman Pat Roberts remarked, "What concerns me most . . . is what appears to be a campaign of press leaks by the CIA in an effort to discredit the president."

A former CIA analyst who now works in another government post and asked not to be named told me, "Langley is predominantly liberal. I would also describe it as too close to the foreign policy establishment. A lot of them came from universities where the foreign relations departments tend to be liberal. That is how a lot of them get hired. Someday, they want to be college professors and members of the Council on Foreign Relations. They basically do not want to be seen as knuckle-draggers. The temptation is to do what the mainstream wants them to do." A White House aide echoed this sentiment: "You have to remember, Langley is like a college faculty and all that that means politically."

What it means, in the words of Senator John McCain, a member of a blue-ribbon committee that investigated CIA shortfalls, is that the CIA is a "rogue agency." Otto Reich, a Cuban-born diplomat who has dedicated his career to opposing Fidel Castro, has also spent years battling the CIA's soft approach toward the dictator. Reich told me, "There were rogue elements in the CIA who did not like Bush foreign policy and did not like Bush people. I think they really have some folks who are patriotic officers who will risk their lives. And they have some liberal professors who believe they are at Harvard and not at Langley."

While CIA bureaucrats have anonymously attacked Bush administration figures through leaks to the press, the CIA was docile during the Clinton years, and even, according to one inside source, punished conservative analysts. Brian Latell, a national intelligence officer for Latin America, stands as an example. He briefed the Senate Foreign Relations Committee in 1993 on ousted Haitian leader Jean-Bertrand Aristide's mental state. Republican senator Jesse Helms used Latell's testimony to bash Clinton, who wanted to restore Aristide to power. Latell found himself transferred to the Center for the Study of Intelligence, from where he retired. "Many of my colleagues laid low or took foreign assignments in 1993 and 1994 to escape the crackdown on conservatives in the agency," the former analyst said.

The irony to Latell, and to other conservatives, is that liberals, longtime foes of CIA operations in the Cold War and Vietnam, have embraced the Agency as the internal opposition organ to Bush.

Just like a college campus, Langley has produced its share of leftist eccentrics. Perhaps the most notable is Ray McGovern, a peace activist who has committed his retirement years to railing against President Bush. He has joined the ranks of professors who write and say that the September 11 attacks were an "inside job" orchestrated by the government.

McGovern served as a senior analyst at the CIA—so senior that he delivered the President's Daily Brief to both the Reagan and George H. W. Bush White Houses. McGovern had access to America's most secret secrets.

Fast-forward twenty years and you find this same fellow at a September 2006 peace rally in Washington. "Is there a cover-up? Yes. The question is what's being covered up," McGovern said of September 11. "Why do you think the vice president let that plane, or whatever it was, hit the Pentagon?" With that statement, McGovern added to conspiracy theorists' argument that the government planned the attack, or willingly allowed it to happen, and left open the possibility that something other than American Flight 77 hit the Pentagon.

McGovern is not the only ex-CIA analyst who spreads conspiracy theories. Another is Bill Christison, who had been a CIA analyst during the Vietnam War. Christison joined McGovern in convening a group of former Langley people who dislike Bush. He said that he had studied footage of the gaping hole in the Pentagon and decided "an airliner almost certainly did not hit the Pentagon." The building "was thus presumably hit by something smaller, possibly a missile or a drone or, less possibly, a smaller manned aircraft." Christison said that the World Trade Center and an adjacent building were not in fact brought down by two airliners, as the commission found. "All three were most probably destroyed by controlled demolition charges placed in the buildings before 9/11." The name of the group Christison and McGovern founded is Veteran Intelligence Professionals for Sanity.

Christison told me he wants the United Nations to investigate September 11 and wants President Bush charged as a criminal. "I think he and Cheney should both be simultaneously impeached for war crimes, for…being responsible for something on the order of 650,000 Iraqi deaths, because of his support of Israel, for supporting the killing of many Palestinians and many Lebanese and for lying in order to get the people of this country to support invading Iraq," he said.

A FAVORITE TACTIC

At the White House, the problem wasn't conspiracy theories, but leaks. Cables written by the CIA station chief in Baghdad, often dire in their assessments, showed up in the *New York Times* just days after reaching Washington. Pentagon officials, long wary of Langley, wondered if CIA officers were writing reports for publication in the *New York Times* or for government policymakers. Thanks to leakers, the *New York Times* also reproduced parts of the National Intelligence Estimate (NIE), the crown jewel of the intelligence community representing the opinions of its premier analysts. The NIE excerpts offered, not coincidentally, the most negative assessments of the wars in Iraq and against al Qaeda.

Another damaging revelation came when someone in the Agency talked to the *Washington Post* about a network of secret holding cells in Europe and elsewhere for captured top al Qaeda leaders (like Khalid Sheikh Mohammed). The leak was an embarrassment not only to the Bush administration but also to cooperating countries that had joined the War on

Terror. And it brought widespread condemnation of a prisoner system outside judicial review. One of the *Post*'s CIA sources for this story was a campaign supporter of Democrat John Kerry, a former agent named Mary
McCarthy.

Then came the mother of all leaks, again on the pages of the *New York
Times*. Under publisher Arthur Sulzberger Jr., the *Times* had become a strident critic of President Bush, Republicans, and the conservative movement
in general. Attacks appeared daily, both on the front page and on the editorial pages. In December 2005, the *Times* disclosed a top-secret program for
instantaneous eavesdropping on suspected terrorists calling someone within
the United States. The administration did not always get court approval for
tapping these calls because timing was crucial: the slightest delay and they
could miss it. The goal was to penetrate an attack like those of September 11
in its infancy.

After all, Ramzi bin al-Sheib, a September 11 plotter, had been denied four
visa requests to enter the United States. Forced to stay put in the Middle East,
he held a series of phone conversations with U.S.-based Mohamed Atta, the
ringleader of the group that hijacked the four airliners. Logic tells you it was
not idle chitchat. If Bush's terror surveillance program had been in place, a
man like bin al-Sheib—who had been denied a visa because of suspected terror links—would likely be on a list of persons to monitor, and his calls to the
United States would have been intercepted. In other words, the September 11
attacks could have been prevented had the intelligence service employed
post–September 11 tools like the terrorist surveillance program. As General
Michael Hayden, who ran the National Security Agency (NSA) in 2001, said,
"Had this program been in effect prior to 9/11, it is my professional judgment
that we would have detected some of the 9/11 al Qaeda operatives in the
United States, and we would have identified them as such."

The *New York Times* story destroyed that advantage. Congressman Hoekstra told me al Qaeda adjusted its tactics after learning how the NSA, the

nation's eavesdropper, operated. "Al Qaeda consciously puts in tactics and strategies that they believe will counter what our capabilities are," he said. "It's very, very clear that when you take a look at how al Qaeda communicates and the techniques that they use, they have become much more sensitive to electronic communication. They know how we may or may not intercept calls. They have figured out certain techniques that many believe will make it much more difficult for us to intercept."

There is another reason the Bush team went mad over leaks. The damage ran deeper. Leaks not only inform the enemy about an ongoing covert operation, but they also send a dangerous signal to potential sources. The CIA has been weak on human (as opposed to technological) intelligence sources—called HUMINT in intelligence circles—and leaks only make the situation worse. Why risk your life and become an agent for the CIA if it can't keep its secrets, if it might reveal you as a source, either directly or because you were the only person capable of passing on the information?

The CIA's job is to collect facts and let the White House, the Pentagon, and the State Department make national security policy. But an agency that is supposed to be scrupulously nonpartisan has become increasingly political—during a time of war—against America's elected commander in chief. Sometimes the opposition is open, and is not just a matter of leaks. A number of senior CIA operators retired from Langley and showed up in the national media as book authors or talking heads in order to attack the Bush administration.

One of the most notable is Michael Scheuer, a CIA analyst in the CIA's bin Laden unit trying to solve the puzzle of al Qaeda. Scheuer wrote *Imperial Hubris: Why the West Is Losing the War on Terror*, a thoroughly Bush-bashing exercise that got him on *60 Minutes*, which became a sort of open mic for Bush opponents. The interviewer never asked Scheuer the logical question of why he and his colleagues at the CIA hadn't caught bin Laden. If the West was losing, weren't analysts like Scheuer partly responsible?

Scheuer was not alone. A number of Agency alumni emerged from Langley's collegial ranks to accuse Bush, in books and articles, of various failures. The ex-analysts and officers criticized Bush for being too cozy with the Saudis, too tough on Iran, too political in his use of intelligence, too incompetent to catch bin Laden, and many other alleged failings. Perhaps the most curious critic is Tyler Drumheller. He spent years in the clandestine service, rising to the post of division chief of all stations in Europe. An officer who rose to such lofty ranks would carry automatic credibility. Drumheller retired, went on network TV, including *60 Minutes*, and told some incredible stories about Bush's deception. They really were incredible, because, according to sources within the CIA, they were not true. They were the work of a storyteller, not a truth teller.

What bothered Hoekstra as much as the leaks and public relations assault was a 2002 intelligence mission to Niger. It was concocted within the bowels of Langley without the knowledge of the White House or even the CIA director. The mission involved sending an anti-Bush partisan to Africa. Former ambassador Joseph Wilson was supposed to find out whether Saddam Hussein had attempted to buy more uranium yellowcake from Niger, as Iraq had done in the 1980s. Yellowcake is an essential component of a nuclear bomb. The trip to sort out a critical prewar intelligence question was even more curious. Wilson wasn't required to sign a confidentiality agreement. In fact, there were no written guidelines for his mission; nor did he file a written report. And the person who got him the trip turned out to be his wife, Valerie Plame, a CIA officer who considered the idea of Iraq approaching Niger as "a crazy report," though it was believed by British intelligence. The trip's fallout embroiled Bush, Vice President Dick Cheney, and chief advisor Karl Rove in an unwarranted political crisis at the very time that they were trying to execute a war.

It was all too much for Congressman Pete Hoekstra. On May 18, 2006, he signed the warning letter to the president. Months later, I asked him about the CIA elements he had mentioned. "Elements?" he answered. "The whole institution is against the president."

In my own investigation for this book, I counted at least eight occasions on which current or former intelligence officials made serious allegations of wrongdoing against the president's men that turned out to be untrue. In each case, the charges were first leaked to the press and became accepted as another blow to the president. Months later the allegations would be proven untrue, but by then the news had moved on. In some cases, even though independent investigations had completely discredited the charges, the press continued to repeat them unchallenged.

In addition to the leaks of unsubstantiated charges, there were at least four politically motivated leaks that revealed classified programs with the dual intent of ending them and damaging the president.

TENET

In April 2007, the CIA struck again. This time it was not an obscure operator like Scheuer or Drumheller raking over the Bush administration. It was the former director himself, George Tenet.

Kept on as director in 2001, brought into the inner circle and given the prestigious Medal of Freedom, Tenet rewarded Bush's loyalty with disloyalty. His memoir, *At the Center of the Storm*, shifts blame for some of the CIA's big mistakes from Agency people to Bush people. Tenet's five-hundred-page gambit, published while Bush remained in office, confirmed for conservatives all that had gone wrong at Langley. New York publishers have reaped millions of dollars publishing "Bush Lied, Troops Died" books. Tenet's book, for which he received a reported $3 million advance, would sell more copies with the Bush team still in office. Tenet followed the money, not historic protocol.

I came to the conclusion while reporting for this book that no federal bureaucracy uses the media so ruthlessly to quiet its perceived political rivals. The CIA owns what the press and everyone in Washington wants: inside information. A leak here and a leak there can slowly pick apart a foe until his effectiveness is gone. Undersecretary for defense Douglas Feith, Senator Pat Roberts, Ambassador John Bolton, CIA director Porter Goss and his staff, White House aide Lewis "Scooter" Libby, and Vice President Dick Cheney are examples of those who challenged the CIA and got beat up, thrown out, or locked up.

Through incompetence, leaks, and false allegations within the CIA, an agency charged with a lead role in the War on Terror, the CIA has become one of President Bush's most damaging political enemies.

CHAPTER 1

WAR BEGINS

"The Director of Central Intelligence shall be responsible for national intelligence.... Such national intelligence should be timely, objective, independent of political considerations."

National Security Act of 1947, creating the CIA

M ichael Maloof was back in the game. He and another Pentagon aide, David Wurmser, drove the short distance from the Pentagon to CIA headquarters in Langley, Virginia. It was early October, a good season in Washington, but the scenic ride along the tree-lined George Washington Parkway could not soothe Maloof's nerves. A big gash still hollowed out one side of the Pentagon, and America was at war. Douglas Feith, the top civilian policy advisor to Defense Secretary Donald Rumsfeld, had summoned him for a big, secret project.

Maloof was a legend within the Pentagon circle that tracked arms proliferation. His office was obscure, but it performed a crucial national security function. The job of the Defense Technology Security Administration (DTSA) was to review proposed exports of U.S. technology and weapons. Maloof and his colleagues took their jobs more seriously than that. They pored over reams of intelligence reports to check out just who might be the ultimate buyer of American satellite technology and other high-tech items with military applications.

Maloof knew about the problems in the CIA. In 1998, for example, a high-ranking commission on ballistic missile threats had wanted to review the CIA's secret assessments, but couldn't get them. There were two problems. First, the Clinton administration's gutting of the Agency had left too few clandestine officers and analysts to track weapons shipments to such rogue states as North Korea and Iran. Second, the CIA refused to share what information it did have. So the commission had turned to Maloof. It was one of his early encounters with Langley and its miserly approach to sharing information.

Maloof had been watching the arms traffic and taking notes, which he passed on to the commission. "Information that Mike provided contained decisive insights on the existence and workings of global proliferation networks," said William Schneider Jr., a commission member who went on to lead the Pentagon's Defense Science Board. "This phenomenon was missed by most of the intelligence community, which then predicted that North Korea would be unable to produce an intercontinental missile threat for fifteen years." Shortly after the commission released its report debunking CIA estimates, the Stalinist North Korean regime launched a two-stage missile. "Mike was an encyclopedia of intelligence," Schneider told me. In contrast, the CIA briefers were near silent. At one commission meeting, a CIA briefer was so reticent that Schneider commented after he left the room, "He doesn't deserve food."

But Maloof fell into hot water with the Clinton administration after helping expose dubious deals between some of America's largest weapons makers and Communist China. This embarrassed the administration, because several of these companies had previously flooded the Democratic Party with campaign cash. Maloof had also helped Congress's bipartisan Cox Commission in its investigations, which revealed an extensive Chinese spying network, defense industry collusion, and an apparent lack of interest in such espionage and arms sales by the Clinton administration. Clinton's political appointees labeled Maloof a leaker to the press. Maloof was ostracized and exiled; the DTSA was removed from the Pentagon and relocated in an office complex in Arlington, Virginia. The Defense Intelligence Agency (DIA) occasionally tapped him for a minor mission, but never anything like the salad days of the 1990s.

But now Douglas Feith, one of the neoconservatives who had captured control of key national security posts in the new George Bush administration, came to the rescue. America was at war with the Taliban and al Qaeda in Afghanistan. But another quarry was moving into target range: Saddam Hussein. Feith wanted Maloof to use his intelligence sleuthing to answer a big question: what were the connections between al Qaeda and other terror groups? "There was a mountain of intelligence on this subject, on terror networks," Feith said later. "I needed someone to digest it. I wanted a policy strategy. It was absolutely not about Saddam and al Qaeda. This was about the entire global network: all terror groups, all state sponsors." It was about other connections as well, including, as Maloof's research would reveal, how al Qaeda skimmed money from the diamond trade in Africa to finance operations.

So Maloof headed out to Langley that October day to get the CIA's cooperation in obtaining years of intelligence reports—intercepts, information from or about al Qaeda sources, foreign intelligence agency assessments—to help answer these questions. Maloof didn't know it at the time, but his trip to Langley marked the first day of the CIA bureaucracy's war on Donald Rumsfeld's Pentagon and George W. Bush's White House.

Maloof and his superiors gradually learned in those first weeks of war that the CIA had never done a terrorist-linkage analysis like what was now required. Paul Wolfowitz, deputy defense secretary and another neoconservative, was appalled at what the CIA analysts had to offer. Observers remember intelligence analysts leaving Wolfowitz's office one October day in a foul mood after a harsh critique. "Nobody thought the intelligence was as good as it could be," Douglas Feith later recalled. "It never is. There was a feeling the CIA was leaving out information to fit preconceived conceptions." A major bone of contention was whether it was possible that Saddam Hussein's regime would cooperate with al Qaeda. The CIA ruled it out of the question, saying that Saddam's secular Ba'athists would never cooperate with Osama bin Laden's fundamentalist Islamic terrorists. The neoconservatives at the Pentagon thought the CIA was operating with a closed mind.

They weren't the only ones at the Pentagon who thought this way. The roots of the Pentagon's mistrust of the CIA went back at least to the Gulf War of 1991. Back then, the CIA had said that Iraq was five years away from building a nuclear bomb. But postwar United Nations inspectors found a much more mature program. It put Baghdad fewer than eighteen months away. Without Desert Storm, the allied operation against Iraq's invasion of Kuwait, Saddam would have controlled a nuclear arsenal by the early 1990s. The CIA's shoddiness had a profound impact on Vice President Dick Cheney, who served as the defense secretary at that time. Aides say he never fully trusted CIA assessments again.

After Desert Storm, Maloof had met with CIA officials to discuss his findings on Western countries, like Germany, supplying Iran with machine tools needed to produce ballistic missiles. Iran was working on the family of Shahab missiles capable of reaching its arch-enemy Israel—and Europe as well. But the CIA told Maloof to get lost. His poking around, they said, jeopardized the CIA's network of Iranian sources in Europe.

□ □ □

At Langley, now a decade later, Maloof was escorted to the agency's Counterterrorism Center (CTC), a top-secret analytical branch that studied intelligence reports on various terror groups and leaders. Maloof met with a number of senior CIA people to explain the intelligence gap and ask for help. The Pentagon wanted years of intelligence reporting on al Qaeda, Iraq, Iran, and other potential targets in the war against global terrorism. The Langley crew listened politely. But at the end, the CTC directors said, simply, no. The CIA, not Feith's policy shop, would do such work—if ordered. There were follow-up requests. Still no. "They wouldn't provide any assistance," Maloof said later. "They would stonewall us."

Finally, Wolfowitz interceded. The DIA pressed the CIA to cooperate. Years of CIA intelligence reports, some mature, others raw and unconfirmed, started arriving at the Pentagon. Maloof and Wurmser set up shop inside the supersecure National Military Intelligence Center on the Pentagon's third floor. By December, they had produced a 150-slide briefing on contacts between al Qaeda, Iraq, and Iran. "The Agency blew a gasket," Maloof recalled.

Maloof and Wurmser's report showed that anti-Americanism was an increasingly sufficient motive for otherwise divergent parties, such as Sunni terrorists, Shi'ite terrorists, and Saddam Hussein's Ba'athists, to collaborate in a terror network. It was a conclusion that the CIA had ruled out.

Said Feith, "There was a general sense of some of these subjects that CIA analysts had theories and hypotheses and preconceptions that we did not share. The CIA should not be filtering out information inconsistent with its own preconceptions."

Maloof did not fully realize at the time how his mission offended the extremely territorial Langley. Wolfowitz and others pushed the CIA to do better, and some in the CIA did not like it. Soon, Democratic lawmakers, principally Senator Carl Levin of Michigan, began charging that Feith had set up an illegal organization. Levin, using the friendly *Washington Post* and *New*

York Times, launched a campaign against a "rogue" intelligence cell inside the Defense Department. Maloof soon realized his long career was in jeopardy, as he had become a political target of the CIA, which was working through the Democrats and the press.

THE CIA DISAPPOINTS

Donald Rumsfeld fumed in his office. While he was preparing a war against al Qaeda and its Taliban hosts in Afghanistan that September, immediately after the attacks on America, his generals were telling him that they lacked adequate intelligence from the CIA.

Rumsfeld pushed his generals, but Air Force General Charles Holland, then in charge of U.S. Special Operations Command, responded each time with the same answer: the CIA had not yet prepared the full battlespace. (Preparing the battlespace means inserting teams to collect intelligence on landing strips, safe houses, and friendly and enemy forces, so the invading force knows as much about the battlespace as possible and knows the best places to land and operate.) Most of the Agency's people positioned themselves in the north, working with the Northern Alliance, an old ally from the 1980s Soviet occupation. It had few personnel, and fewer human sources, in the south, where most al Qaeda and Taliban factions operated. Taliban leader Mullah Omar and Osama bin Laden himself moved from camp to camp in that area. The CIA, under director George Tenet, had not put together a cohesive operation. The job fell to Army Green Berets, who pulled together tribal leaders like Hamid Karzai as quickly as possible.

The CIA, meanwhile, had leaked information to the Washington press about a supposedly crack paramilitary force that was preparing to fight the War on Terror in Afghanistan. The several hundred–strong force of six separate units would penetrate Afghanistan and prepare the landscape for contingents of special operations forces and pro-U.S. Afghanis. This leak was purely a back-patting exercise—and, as Rumsfeld knew, the back-patting was not deserved.

The Pentagon, however, had swiftly moved the carrier *Kitty Hawk* off the coast of Pakistan and was doing some leaking of its own. But unlike the CIA, it was doing it for diplomatic and military reasons. The *Kitty Hawk*, anonymous sources said, would become a floating base for Army Special Forces (Green Beret) A-Teams, Delta Force, and special night-flying aircraft. The storyline was mostly a fiction meant to cover for President Pervez Musharraf of Pakistan. Musharraf did not want his people to know the extent of his collaboration with the Americans, for fear it would anger Pakistan's own radical Muslims. In reality, most U.S. Special Forces flew into Pakistan, set up base camps, and prepared for war. The U.S. used Pakistan's air bases, and the CIA launched its Hellfire-armed Predator drone from Musharraf's soil.

Another fiction was that U.S. Green Berets supposedly flew into southern Afghanistan, joined tribal leader Hamid Karzai, and drove toward Kandahar, the Taliban's birthplace. The true story is less romantic. The Americans brought Karzai, the future Afghani leader, out of Afghanistan and into Pakistan, where they armed and trained his men. And when the invasion came, the joint force would reenter the country as one.

Finally, Rumsfeld ordered the invasion, whether the CIA was ready or not. The war began on October 7, 2001, putting on display a new kind of unconventional conflict. Air power, a few hundred commandos, and local Afghanis liberated the country. Still, the Pentagon considers the CIA's prewar work in southern Afghanistan a failure. The vaunted CIA paramilitary force that received so much prewar hype was in fact ill trained, ill equipped, a bit long in the tooth, and in the end needed to be bailed out by the Army. War planners had furiously signed scores of secret orders transferring Army Special Forces to the CIA paramilitaries so that they could fight. It was a classified rescue mission never leaked to the press.

As attention turned to Iraq in 2002, Rumsfeld saw more CIA deficiencies. There were virtually no CIA-recruited spies inside Iraq, much less inside Saddam's inner circle, and the CIA's information on the regime was pitiful. For. instance, the CIA did not know that Iraq's power grid, water system, and oil infrastructure had fallen into disrepair.

From bases in northern Iraq, CIA officers hastily tried to make up for lost time and recruit spies from Saddam's regime. A few Special Security Operation members were found, but proved unreliable. They reported spotting Saddam arriving at Dora Farms, a summer home south of Baghdad, and the White House quickly ordered an air strike. But Saddam had never been there on that night.

Rumsfeld tried to compensate for the CIA shortfalls. Commanders inserted more than a thousand special operations troops inside Iraq to spy and to prepare the battlespace. Scores of them roamed the city of Baghdad itself.

Problems with the CIA extended to Iraq war-planning sessions, according to a secret 2003 Joint Chiefs of Staff study I obtained. This study reveals "DoD-CIA disconnects" that "occurred at the strategic and operational level." The study shows that the CIA was keeping such a "close hold on intelligence information" that "some significant planning issues could not be discussed" at the Executive Steering Group, a gaggle of war planners meeting under the guise of the White House National Security Council.

One reason for this was that no doctrine existed governing how the CIA and the Department of Defense were supposed to work together. And there were no procedures for synchronizing "covert information" operations—planting propaganda in enemy media—with public information operations.

Like Dick Cheney, Rumsfeld had doubts about the CIA that predated September 11. He had gotten an eye-opening reminder while heading the 1998 ballistic missile commission that had been briefed by Maloof. Rumsfeld found the CIA's analysis weak. Too often, analysts covering the same subject in different countries didn't share information. He knew, too, that the CIA had missed the maturation of Iraq's nuclear weapons program in 1991. After his experience with the missile convention, he concluded that Langley was underestimating our enemies' capability to strike the U.S. with intercontinental missiles.

Rumsfeld's experience with the ballistic missile commission, coupled with the CIA's lackluster performance in the run-up to the wars in Afghanistan and Iraq, had a lasting impact on him. He quickly moved to expand the Pentagon's intelligence collection capabilities. If the CIA could not prepare a battlespace or find al Qaeda, his own troops would. He signed a top-secret directive to General Charles Holland in July 2002. "The objective is to capture terrorists for interrogation or, if necessary, to kill them, not simply to arrest them in a law enforcement exercise," he wrote.

Rumsfeld created the Pentagon's first undersecretary of defense for intelligence that month. To run it, he tapped his most trusted aide, Stephen Cambone. Green Beret hubs at Fort Bragg, North Carolina, and Fort Lewis, Washington, opened spy schools for commandos. In a bolder move, Rumsfeld won an interagency battle to place Green Berets and a special spy unit known as Task Force Orange inside U.S. embassies in al Qaeda–infested countries, especially on the Horn of Africa. The mission: look around, develop contacts, and report back to Special Operations Command.

At the Pentagon, Rumsfeld's own version of the CIA, the Defense Intelligence Agency, got more money and power. The overall staff shot up to number 7,500. With congressional approval, Rumsfeld empowered the DIA to recruit spies from inside the United States. Who better to penetrate a terror cell than a loyal Arab American? The new cloak-and-dagger operation adopted an unassuming, bureaucratic name: the Defense HUMINT Management Office. Rumsfeld also authorized a number of military spying programs, some done through third parties, that I will not disclose.

While the CIA's failures in Afghanistan were lost on the press, the 9-11 Commission took secret testimony from the Agency and military officials on the paramilitary groups' performance. Like Rumsfeld, the panel was not impressed: "Before 9-11, the CIA did not invest in developing a robust capability to conduct paramilitary operations with U.S. personnel. It relied on proxies instead, organized by CIA operatives without the requisite military training. The results were unsatisfactory." The commission recommended that the Pentagon take over the Agency's much-maligned force, but Rumsfeld refused. He had his own special operators.

"There was tension, especially in the Afghanistan campaign, on this idea of readiness," recalled William Schneider. "How ready are they to conduct operations in a specific area?"

Henry A. Crumpton, a longtime spy, led the CIA campaign in Afghanistan from the war's start. He generally gave his people high marks. But Crumpton found that his paramilitary force had deteriorated during the Clinton administration, shrinking to a core force of a "few dozen." "Most . . . lacked relevant language skills, experience in central Asia, and expertise in counterterrorism," Crumpton wrote in the 2005 book *Transforming U.S. Intelligence.* "Moreover, CIA operations officers with the requisite qualifications often had limited or rusty tactical skills."

Later, a senior Pentagon official commented, "If SOF [special operations forces] hadn't pulled CIA's chestnuts out of the fire, Tenet would have been gone much earlier."

In his memoir, *At the Center of the Storm*, Tenet makes some extraordinary claims about CIA feats in southern Afghanistan in 2001, which are challenged by at least one eyewitness. The claims revolve around a CIA officer, "Greg V.," who was assigned to future Afghanistan president Hamid Karzai. Greg V. was part of a small CIA unit that hooked up with an Army Green Beret A-Team. The Special Forces soldiers trained Karzai's men and fought with them in a push toward Kandahar, the Taliban stronghold. Tenet writes of a decisive November 17 battle around Tarin Kowt:

Greg V. took command of the situation, sprinting from one defensive position to another, telling the Afghans that this was their chance to prove their worth and make history. "If necessary, die like men," he shouted....

Had Karzai's position been overrun, as appeared likely for much of November 17, the entire future of the Pashtun rebellion in the south could have ended.

When I read this excerpt to the eyewitness (a very reliable source on military matters in the years I've known him), he laughed heartily. The source said Greg V. had been at base headquarters during the entire battle.

"They could not have gotten that from Greg. Greg would not say those things," the eyewitness said. "None of our guerrillas spoke English," he added. Only Karzai was fluent. That speech would have fallen on deaf ears."

A few pages later, Tenet credits Greg V. with saving Karzai's life during the December 5 "friendly fire" bombing of the A-Team's position north of Kandahar. A team member called in the wrong coordinates and a B-52 put a satellite-guided two-thousand-pound bomb in the wrong place. Three Army soldiers died. "Karzai might have too, if Greg V. hadn't thrown himself on him, knocking him to the ground just as the bombs struck," Tenet writes in *At the Center of the Storm.*

When I read this excerpt to the eyewitness, he laughed again. He said Karzai had been in a relatively sturdy building about one hundred yards from the blast. The explosion shook the structure, knocking a cascade of debris to the floor. Karzai suffered a small cut on his cheek. Greg V. was not hurt.

"That's an awesome piece of fiction," the source said. Of the CIA's performance alongside the A-Team, he said, "Their role would have been handing off their contacts. But they had none. They set up receivers and sent reports."

PENTAGON PAPERS

Douglas Feith's operation and Rumsfeld's homegrown spying network grated on CIA headquarters. While ideological differences did exist between the two camps, the true rub was bureaucratic territorialism. Analysts jealously guarded their turf. Now Rumsfeld's men were forcing the analytical branch to do hard analysis on al Qaeda, a group the intelligence gatherers had not detected until 1997—years after its formation. The Pentagon was now competing with the CIA to recruit the best spies. The Agency was no longer the only game in town, and it wasn't too happy. The CIA's anti-Pentagon culture began to reveal itself in the writings of former employees, including former director Robert Gates. "More than a few CIA veterans—including me—are unhappy about the dominance of the Defense Department in the intelligence arena and the decline in the CIA's central role," Gates, who would succeed Rumsfeld as defense secretary, wrote in the *New York Times*. "I publicly opposed the establishment of the [director of national intelligence]. But the change has been made, and we who were in the CIA during its halcyon days must adjust to a new world."

By 2002, Maloof's recommendations for improving the nation's anti-terrorism strategies had evolved. Another two-person team, DIA officer Tina Shelton and Christopher Carney, a Navy Reserve intelligence officer who would go on to win election to Congress as a Democrat, continued the terror network analysis. Shelton and Carney did business as the Policy Counterterrorism Evaluation Group, and they were able to point out networks linking terror groups. Meanwhile, unbeknownst to Feith, Wolfowitz put one of his aides to work developing a briefing focused only on Saddam Hussein and al Qaeda. Eventually, all three projects—Maloof's, Carney's, and Wolfowitz's—melded into one product. This provided an alternative view to the CIA's about the relations among terror networks and Middle Eastern states. Using the same material—the decades of intelligence reporting gathered by the CIA—the Pentagon painted a different picture. The Maloof-Carney-Wolfowitz picture depicted stronger al Qaeda–Baghdad ties than did Langley's.

Feith took the combined report and began a series of briefings on its findings, first to Rumsfeld, then to about thirty officers at the CIA (including Tenet), then to Stephen Hadley at the National Security Council, and then finally to Vice President Cheney. Tenet later remarked that he did not think much of the paper and relied on it little when he wrote his own assessment.

In his book, Tenet did not hide his disgust for Feith and for what he called "Team Feith." He recalled sitting in on the Feith briefing and thinking, "This is complete crap, and I want this to end right now." He accused Feith of orchestrating "cherry-picked, selective data" from his agency's years of raw intelligence reports on a connection between al Qaeda and Iraq.

Yet Tenet's own analysis of the relationship, which he put in writing in a 2002 letter to the Senate Intelligence Committee, stated, "Iraq's increasing support to extremist Palestinians, coupled with growing indications of a relationship with al Qaeda, suggest that Baghdad's links to terrorists will increase, even absent U.S. military action . . . We have solid reporting of senior-level contacts between Iraq and al Qaeda going back a decade . . . . We have credible reporting that al Qaeda leaders sought contacts in Iraq who could help them acquire WMD capabilities."

Feith's al Qaeda research reflected just a fraction of his workload. At the Pentagon, everything—budgets, deployment orders, policies, laws, procurements—passed through his desk on the way to the defense secretary. Feith often began work at 7 a.m. and did not leave until 8 p.m. or later. Sometimes he took Air Force brigadier general Ron Yaggi, his military assistant, along on the limo ride home to go over a stack of papers. Feith had fired his first military aide, a colonel, whom his staff found too abrasive. Yaggi had worked for Clinton's policy people and knew how to be diplomatic. He also knew how to get things done, provide advice, and push paper.

The Pentagon was deploying units at a fast pace. Feith had to review each Joint Staff Form 136, which justified the troop movements. "I don't ever recall him having a leisurely lunch," Yaggi recalled. "It was always a working lunch." Rumsfeld was a tough boss. Feith would return from meetings with his head low, the victim of another chewing-out. If he used the word *very* in a memo, Rumsfeld made him justify the adverb. But Feith, a protégé of Reagan hardliner Richard Perle, rolled with the punches. He soon forged a close relationship with the naturally suspicious Rumsfeld and won a seat at his decision-making "round table." Given all that he did at the Pentagon, Feith later expressed consternation that a few hundred pages of terrorist-group assessments, focusing on al Qaeda's documented connections with Iraq, would draw such strident attacks from Democrats and come to dominate talk of his legacy.

Feith's shop began hearing rumors from Langley. His men, went the quip, were practicing intelligence without a license. Congressional defense aides passed word that the CIA was not really anti-Bush, but rather insecure and thin-skinned. Its reaction to the Defense Department's intelligence efforts was not to regard the work as a joint project to defeat America's enemies, but as a threat to its turf. And it lashed out. As Feith, Maloof, and others planned the War on Terror in 2001, they had no idea that some at the CIA were planning another kind of war: a political turf war, using Democratic allies in Congress and a compliant Washington press to target the Pentagon.

SPECIAL PLANS

In 2002, the White House sent word to the Pentagon to start preparing war plans for Iraq. Feith decided that such a huge task demanded unique attention. His top advisor on the Middle East was William Luti, a retired Navy captain and former aide to Newt Gingrich, who served as deputy undersecretary for Near Eastern/South Asian affairs. When Rumsfeld said he wanted his commanders "leaning forward" in the War on Terror, Luti took him seriously. Among Rumsfeld's acolytes, there was none more loyal, hard-charging, or, some would say, grating. Feith and Luti decided to create a new department, the Office of Special Plans, and added thirteen officers to the one who had been working on Iraq. Soon the new office began putting out classified papers on Iraq. Luti later concluded that the moniker was their first mistake. The term "Special Plans" conjured up for opponents of the war all sorts of nefarious conspiracy theories, and sooner or later those theories would make their way to the front pages.

Luti's status entitled him to the CIA's senior executive brief, a somewhat watered-down version of the President's Daily Brief. A briefer would show up at a set time and deliver the goods. But after a while, Luti and other war hardliners noticed a pattern. If they questioned a CIA assessment (such as "Muslim Shi'ites and Sunnis don't work together"), they would get a defensive response. Some of the things they said to briefers became the stuff of negative gossip throughout Langley's collegial analytical branch. Worse, some tidbits showed up in the press. After a while, Luti and other senior policymakers either sat silent and expressionless during the briefing or declined the in-person briefing altogether, taking a written report instead. The Pentagon's distrust of the CIA had grown so deep that the critical relationship of intelligence briefer to policymaker disintegrated.

With the Taliban ousted from Kabul, Rumsfeld turned to the global war and how to fight it. He was not totally happy with the plans delivered from U.S. Special Operations Command, which he would anoint a year later as the war's global commanding force. So he turned instead to his policy shop, principally the assistant secretary of defense for special operations and low-intensity conflict, to submit a plan for how commandos could be deployed around the world at a moment's notice to wipe out al Qaeda cells. By the summer, he was signing a secret order telling them to do just that. Rumsfeld also summoned an old friend, William Schneider Jr., to his E-Ring office in the Pentagon. He had wanted Schneider, with whom he had worked in the 1970s, to be his deputy secretary or policy chief. But Schneider preferred to retain his consulting business, so Rumsfeld handed him a plum position: chairman of the Defense Science Board, an influential advisory group.

Rumsfeld told Schneider he wanted the board's ideas on how to wage a worldwide conflict with particular emphasis on military intelligence. "Intelligence needed to break away from stovepipes and become more joint," Schneider told me later, which in intelligence lingo means that intelligence needed to be less narrowly compartmentalized and better shared. "We needed centralized processing centers, target information fed quickly to pilots and ground commanders." The focus needed to be on special operations forces. "It was not practicable to operate against these foreign operators with traditional forces," he said, adding, "everybody needed to be a collector" of intelligence.

In late summer 2002, Schneider's panel produced a study called "Special Operations and Joint Forces in Support of Countering Terrorism." Like the policy shop's plan, it was a civilian panel's blueprint for how to fight the new, stateless enemy. And it made the CIA nervous. The CIA, Schneider told me, had been slow to distribute information to field commanders. There was, he said, "institutional conflict with feeding the operators with the same sense of urgency that operators feel are necessary."

Schneider's paper called for developing "new capabilities, sources, and methods to enable deep penetration of adversaries" and creating "a surge capability in intelligence to preempt and deal with rapidly emerging crises." It likened finding al Qaeda cells to the cat-and-mouse game played by submarines during the Cold War.

Schneider's report guided Rumsfeld's efforts to make the Defense Intelligence Agency and special operations larger, and to make them more involved in intelligence collection.

Bush's people had no idea in those heady post–September 11 days that their campaign to find and kill al Qaeda terrorists would spawn an inquisition on Capitol Hill. Nor could they imagine that some Democrats would want them charged as criminals.

CHAPTER 2

ADVICE AND CONSENT

"There has been some debate over how 'imminent' a threat Iraq poses. I do believe that Iraq poses an imminent threat, but I also believe that after September 11, that question is increasingly outdated. It is in the nature of these weapons, and the way they are targeted against civilian populations, that documented capability and demonstrated intent may be the only warning we get. To insist on further evidence could put some of our fellow Americans at risk. Can we afford to take that chance? We cannot!"

Senator Jay Rockefeller, in a floor speech justifying his vote to authorize force to remove Saddam Hussein on October 10, 2002

In late 2003, the CIA's war on the Pentagon—and on the White House—shifted to the secure hearing rooms of the Senate Intelligence Committee. The committee had begun the most extensive investigation of the CIA since the Church hearings of the 1970s. During these hearings, Democratic senator Frank Church had publicly probed and scolded the CIA over all sorts of misdeeds in the shadow of the Cold War.

This time, most of the probing would occur behind closed doors. The committee first looked at why the CIA had failed to penetrate the September 11 plot. It then examined prewar intelligence on Iraq and why the CIA had gotten it wrong. An October 2002 National Intelligence Estimate had said Saddam Hussein still possessed stockpiles of chemical weapons and was reconstituting his nuclear weapons program. Post-Saddam inspections found no stockpiles and no restarted atomic research. The committee was also parsing President Bush's 2003 State of the Union address. In making a case for war, the president had quoted British intelligence sources' claim that Iraq had made inquiries about buying uranium from an unnamed African country. Later, the White House acknowledged that its own intelligence services lacked confidence in the British analysis and should have knocked those sixteen words out of the speech.

The Senate Intelligence Committee had a long tradition of bipartisanship, overseeing the CIA and fifteen other intelligence agencies. But in 2003, with a presidential election a year away, that comity fell apart. It became clear that Democrats were going to use the committee as a weapon against Bush. Relations between the chairman, Kansas Republican Pat Roberts, and the top-ranking Democrat, Jay Rockefeller of West Virginia, soured fast.

The two senators already stood as contrasts in the American patchwork quilt. Rockefeller had a polite, professorial manner. He had inherited money and a blue-blood aura from his great-grandfather, oil magnate John D. Rockefeller, once the richest man in America. The great-grandson moved to Emmons, West Virginia, as a VISTA (Volunteers In Service To America) volunteer, fell in love with the state's rural ways, and settled down.

Rockefeller's inherited millions did not stop him from starting at the bottom of the political food chain. He won elections as a state delegate, West Virginia's secretary of state, and governor. Worth $200 million, he spent $12 million of it to win his Senate seat in 1984, the year of Ronald Reagan's landslide reelection. Once in Washington, he disdained raw partisan politics. But circumstances change. The Democrats had grown tired of being in the minority. A scandal over Iraqi weapons would thrill the Washington press corps and perhaps defeat Bush's reelection bid. According to one of his staffers, Rockefeller's metamorphosis into a partisan firebrand was the work of Senator Carl Levin. Levin, a veteran liberal lawmaker, was Rockefeller's colleague on the Intelligence Committee and the ranking Democrat on the Senate Armed Services Committee, which is responsible for overseeing the Pentagon. Levin's staff funneled a wealth of rumors and allegations to Democrats on the Intelligence Committee that seemed to justify aggressive investigations.

Pat Roberts is a gruff former Marine who supported President Bush but privately complained about the administration's incompetence. His great-grandfather was a gun- and Bible-toting newspaper man who had started the *Oskaloosa Independent*. Roberts worked for various Kansas politicians before winning his own congressional seat in 1980. Where Rockefeller was urbane and measured, Roberts personified the Kansas prairie and its straight-talking, hardworking inhabitants.

The two were getting on less well in private than in public. Roberts noticed a troubling trend from his once-gentlemanly vice chairman. The two would talk over schedules and witnesses and hammer out an agreement. Rockefeller would then go to the press and slam the investigation, accusing Republicans of stalling for political reasons. When Roberts confronted him, Rockefeller would say, "Oh, don't worry about that," as if the twenty-year Washington veteran did not know how Beltway politics worked.

Rockefeller would sometimes sink to locker-room chitchat, bringing up his bowel movements in closed committee meetings. "I just had the most magnificent shit," he remarked one day to Roberts as the session was about to begin.

During the committee investigations, an internal memo surfaced that revealed the Democrats' brutal political aims. Written by a Rockefeller staffer, the unsigned paper laid out a political strategy that could not be described as finding the truth. It was basically this: use the committee to press investigations as far they could go; leak promising leads to the media; and then, regardless of what the committee finds, demand another investigation into the same matters by an independent body—and do it on a schedule that coincides with the election.

"Prepare to launch an independent investigation when it becomes clear we have exhausted the opportunity to usefully collaborate with the majority," the memo said. "We can pull the trigger on an independent investigation at any time—but we can only do so once."

Even though the investigation had yet to reach any conclusions, the memo advised Democrats to criticize the final report, whatever it would say: "Castigate the majority for seeking to limit the scope of the inquiry. The Democrats will then be in a strong position to reopen the question of establishing an independent commission."

On how to handle Roberts, the memo instructed: "Pull the majority along as far as we can on issues that may lead to major new disclosures regarding improper or questionable conduct by administration officials. . . . We don't know what we will find but our prospects for getting the access we seek is far greater when we have the backing of the majority."

Conservative pundits, including radio talk-show host Sean Hannity, who broke the story, hit the ceiling. FOX News commentator (and later White House press secretary) Tony Snow said the memo "suggests some Senate Democrats wanted to trick their Republican colleagues into mounting a political hit on the president." Enraged, Roberts shut down the investigation. "I was stunned by this memo, shocked by this memo," he told Snow. "We have a thirty-year history in the intelligence committee of nonpartisan activity. . . . What this memo has done is really poisoned the well." At the Pentagon, some termed it the end of the intelligence committee "as we know it."

The turmoil wasn't confined to the Senate side of Capitol Hill. In the House, Democratic leader Nancy Pelosi, soon to be House Speaker, wanted Democrats on Pete Hoekstra's House Intelligence Committee to act like their counterparts in the Senate. She thought Congresswoman Jane Harman, a

California colleague and the top committee Democrat, was a lightweight. Harman was too bipartisan. She did not demand investigations and was not critical enough of the administration in her television appearances. "Pelosi and Harman hate each other," a Republican congressman said. "California is not big enough for both of them."

Pelosi, as House minority leader, was an ex-officio committee member. But her duties as party leader and chief Bush-basher did not provide her enough time to sit in on committee meetings. Still, she had informants who kept her abreast of Harman's conduct, and she did not like what she heard. When the Democrats took the House in 2006, Pelosi got her revenge: one of her first acts as Speaker was to snub Harman, who was in line to become chairman, and give Congressman Silvestre Reyes of Texas the chairmanship. Reyes promptly revealed himself a true intelligence and foreign policy lightweight when he told *Congressional Quarterly* that al Qaeda (which is nearly 100 percent and often stridently Sunni) was primarily a Shi'ite group. A CIA officer wondered aloud to me, "What was he doing during all those War on Terror briefings?"

SNOWE AND HAGEL

The Rockefeller memo highlighted two facts. First, the Democrats planned to cash in on the CIA probe and spend the chips on presidential politics. Second, Roberts did not have a functioning majority on the committee. Balky Republicans Chuck Hagel of Nebraska and Olympia Snowe of Maine often voted with the Democrats. Roberts's lack of a cohesive majority meant that he did not have the votes to permanently halt proceedings.

The probe cranked back up after a few weeks. The committee staff resumed summoning scores of witnesses behind closed doors. A number of intelligence analysts soon realized the panel's secretive deliberations were a great way to get back at the Bush administration. They began making serious allegations—albeit unsubstantiated—against Donald Rumsfeld's Pentagon.

Someone had leaked to the press that CIA analysts were being pressured by senior Pentagon officials concerning the Agency's reports on a link between Saddam Hussein and al Qaeda. But those press reports proved bogus. No analyst who briefed Pentagon policymakers complained to the committee. "The committee found that this process [the policymakers' probing questions] actually improved the Central Intelligence Agency's products," the final Senate report said.

Another charge had come from a retired Defense Intelligence Agency (DIA) analyst (whom the committee refused to identify) working with Rockefeller's staff. The retiree provided the name of a DIA officer who, he said, would tell the committee he was pressured by William Luti of the Office of Special Plans. By this time the hawkish Luti was already a favorite target of *New Yorker* writer Seymour Hersh.

The *Washington Post* reported on the accusation and claimed the DIA analyst had sharply disagreed with Luti on the threat posed by Iraq. But when the analyst himself testified before the committee, he said he had never had such a conversation with Luti. The analyst said he did have two disagreements with him: Luti did not like his use of the word *assassination* when Israel killed terrorist leaders, and Luti once demanded more information on the war in Afghanistan rather than an Israeli-Palestinian casualty count.

Foiled with that witness, the ex-DIA officer working for Rockefeller produced a second witness, another DIA analyst. This person would supposedly nail Luti and the Office of Special Plans by testifying that Luti had pressured him to change some of his assessments. But again the Democrats struck out. When this supposedly important anti-Luti witness showed up for a committee interview, he told staff that Luti "asked tough questions and pressured analysts to have the intelligence to back up what they were saying, but never pressured them to come up with judgments to match preconceived notions."

That final Senate report, signed by Rockefeller, concluded that there had been no pressure to change intelligence reporting on Iraq or on al Qaeda, or to change the Iraq NIE or any other intelligence reports. Instead, the document overflowed with accounts of the CIA's deceit and mistakes. As for Douglas Feith's Office of Special Plans, investigators said its work did not influence the CIA's own 2002 "Iraqi Support for Terrorism" report on the terrorist ties to Saddam Hussein's regime. Not only did the Senate report not find undue pressure on CIA analysts, but it also pointed out that their exclusive school, the Sherman Kent School of Intelligence Analysis, teaches them to expect and field rigorous questions from policymakers. "If we judge or leave open to interpretation that repeated questioning and challenging of intelligence assessments is inappropriate," wrote five Republican committee members, "we do ourselves a disservice as United States senators and limit our own ability to demand rigorous review of intelligence."

In other words, the allegations spread as gospel by intelligence officers throughout the media were unwarranted and unfounded.

The Democrats won nonetheless. The Bush administration acceded to a new investigation, this time by a commission headed by former Democratic senator Chuck Robb and appeals court judge Laurence Silberman. In 2005 the commission concluded, like the Senate panel had, that there had been no political pressure by Bush aides to fix prewar intelligence reports. The Robb-Silberman commission was quickly forgotten by the news media as new CIA officers came forward to make the same allegations in the following months—this time against the White House.

The Democrats won in another way too. In their zeal to attack the Bush administration, the Democrats on the Senate Intelligence Committee simply ignored their own report. Rockefeller appeared with Roberts at a July 9, 2004, press conference on the final report, and, unprompted, laid into Douglas Feith, accusing him of "running a private intelligence failure [sic], which is not lawful." Roberts was stunned, given that the report had exonerated Feith. But here was his vice chairman, standing right next to him, leveling such a charge as if it *were* in the report.

A sitting senator accusing the Defense Department's number-three official of lawbreaking did not go over well across the Potomac. After much soul-searching by Rumsfeld's staff, they decided to send an extraordinary message to Rockefeller: put up or shut up. "On behalf of the department, I request that, if you have any evidence supporting the serious charge you floated during your press conference, you provide it to the department," wrote Powell A. Moore, then the Pentagon's top official for congressional relations. "If there is not evidence, then a retraction and apology would be appropriate.... The department is surprised and disturbed by the assertion during your press conference.... In the course of a year of investigations into activities of the office of the undersecretary of defense for policy [Feith], no one on the committee staff, to my knowledge, has charged that anything unlawful had been done."

The letter was unique. A cabinet-level department does not often take on a powerful senator, especially one who can influence defense dollars and hold up political appointments. But there was no retraction or apology from Rockefeller.

After reporters pored over the landmark 511-page report, it was clear that the explosive Rockefeller memo of a year ago had been played out to perfection. The memo had advised Democrats to "castigate the majority for seeking to limit the scope of the inquiry" even though no report had yet been written. Rockefeller, Levin, and Senator Richard Durbin wrote an "additional views" document attached to the report. "Regrettably, the report paints an incomplete picture of what occurred during this period of time," the three asserted.

LEVIN'S METHODS

Carl Levin's passion for investigating intelligence lapses in the Bush administration contrasted with his conduct during the Clinton years. In the case of John Deutch, Levin had worked to successfully block a committee investigation. It happened this way.

The CIA discovered that in 1997 Deutch, then CIA director, badly mis-
handled highly classified intelligence documents in his laptop computer. It
was up to Tenet, then deputy director, to handle the case. Here, some on the
panel believed, Tenet made serious mistakes. He did not refer the case to the
Justice Department for a criminal probe, but instead—in another example
of CIA territorialism—appointed Nora Slatkin, one of Deutch's close aides,
to investigate. Tenet did not ask what information had been compromised or
order a damage assessment.

Senate Republicans and their staffs wanted to conduct a probe and write
a report. At this point, Levin intervened. At closed committee business meetings, he argued that Tenet was too busy to have delved into the case and
should not be held accountable. Every time the issue was raised, Levin
opposed an investigation. As the Democrats on the committee looked to the
combative Levin for signals on what to do, the probe garnered little support.
Tenet also had a few allies on the GOP side. There was not a majority to
authorize an investigation, and Republicans dropped the matter. "We wanted
to criticize Tenet's role," said a Republican. "Levin would not agree to language that would cast any pale on Tenet."

With this successful stonewall, Levin may have changed history. A report
critical of Tenet's handling of an important case would have become part of
his personnel file. Such damage could have taken him out of the running to
be George W. Bush's first CIA director.

But while Levin was indulgent toward Tenet, he was vicious in striking out
at Bush administration appointees like Feith. He railed against Feith and his
staff for questioning CIA analysts' products. He said such scrutiny amounted
to intimidation, an attempt to force them to change their analyses. During
the closed 2003–2004 committee probe, any time he heard a CIA witness say
the word *pressure* he would exclaim, "Aha: pressure." He thought he had a
smoking gun. Republicans would retort that the witness was referring to
pressure to do better analysis, not political pressure.

Levin exerted his own pressure in the closed committee meetings. Using his trademark prosecutorial style, the senator, peering at the witness over half-rimmed reading glasses, tried to poke holes in assessments with which he did not agree. "He criticized analysts all the time," said a Republican. "Levin was pressing the analysts to say what he wanted them to say. The committee quizzes analysts just like it did not want the Pentagon to do."

No issue brought more Levin cross-examinations than the question of Iraq's weapons of mass destruction. During the debate on an Iraq war resolution, he became convinced that the Bush administration had withheld information from United Nations weapons inspectors. The CIA, he believed, held back its list of promising potential WMD sites. The committee summoned CIA officers for closed sessions to explain how they ranked suspected weapons sites in 2002–2003 and which ones they had shared with the UN. It touched off hours of circular debate, as Levin attacked the very system the CIA used and attempted to impose his views for how each site should have been ranked. Sites ranked low-priority and not shared with the UN should have been in another category, he argued.

Levin voted against the October 2002 Senate resolution authorizing Bush to oust Saddam. It was not because he did not believe Saddam had weapons. It was because he believed the administration was hiding the best sites from UN inspectors in order to press for war rather than further inspections.

But the committee's final bipartisan report found no such deception. There were often plausible explanations as to why the Bush administration did not share data about some sites. For one, the UN team at one point told the CIA to stop sending data. The inspectors were overwhelmed. The committee produced a scorecard. Of 148 known or suspected weapons sites, 44 were not shared. Some high-priority sites were already known to the UN so there was no need to share. Others had not yet been located.

"The Central Intelligence Agency fulfilled the intent of the administration's policy in the sharing of intelligence information," the Senate report concluded.

LUTI'S LIBERTARIAN

One of the most celebrated critics of the defense policy shop was one of William Luti's own subordinates. Luti needed a desk officer to monitor developments in North Africa, and the Pentagon bureaucracy coughed up Air Force lieutenant colonel Karen Kwiatkowski. She boasted an impressive resume, including a stint at the intelligence community's most sacred outpost, the code-breaking National Security Agency (NSA). She also harbored some eccentric libertarian views that her supervisors would find odd. She was antiwar. She opposed U.S. "imperialism." She was suspicious of even the most routine meetings. She did not like Luti. She referred to Bush as "the so-called commander in chief." Only a congressional declaration of war would make him a genuine "commander in chief," she said.

As a desk officer, Kwiatkowski was not a member of Luti's or Feith's inner circle or part of the Office of Special Plans. But she claimed to have a sharp ear for conspiracies. In 2002 she began to disseminate her views—first in an anonymous blog under the pen name "Deep Throat," and then to Seymour Hersh of the *New Yorker*, who was an ardent foe of Bush and his policymakers. Hersh claimed that Luti and his staff referred to themselves as "the cabal." Luti denied this to a *New Yorker* fact checker, saying no one could recall ever hearing the word. But Hersh and the *New Yorker* ran with it anyway.

Hersh wrote that the Office of Special Plans was bypassing the CIA and collecting its own intelligence. He wrote that Luti's relatively tiny office of twenty people was replacing the much larger DIA and CIA. In truth, Hersh or his source confused Special Plans with Maloof's two-man team. It worked outside Luti's office, not in it, and did not collect its own intelligence, but reviewed existing reports. (A 2007 Pentagon inspector general's report would confirm this.) Luti later came to realize that the myth that Feith's office collected intelligence—and all the heat that myth kindled in the press and Senator Levin—had started right outside his office door. Kwiatkowski, Hersh, and the left-wing blogosphere were trying to conjure an Office of Special Conspiracies out of the Office of Special Plans.

Kwiatkowski's blog, "Deep Throat Returns: Insider Notes from the Pentagon," appeared on the website of Colonel David Hackworth. Hackworth, who died in 2005, was a highly decorated Vietnam combat veteran who dabbled in journalism as a military watchdog. His website was open to whistleblowers. In 2002, Kwiatkowski expressed doubts about the intelligence on Iraq's WMD. The charge was substantial, and true, but most of her entries read as personal attacks.

She particularly detested neoconservatives, former House Speaker Newt Gingrich, her boss, Douglas Feith, and Rumsfeld. "Feith's statement that the United States has no interest in running someone else's country is kind of disingenuous," she wrote. "But when the neoconservative leaders of the war party (and we're all invited) say it, well, this thought comes to mind. Those lying bastards!" She added, "Maybe the new imperialism will give retired guys and gals second career opportunities as permanent advisors to governors and mayors and chiefs of police." She called Luti's office "A Mad Hatter's Tea Party."

Kwiatkowski later acknowledged to me that as a military officer she was breaking the law by ridiculing Bush, Cheney, and other leaders. "I'm making jokes about Cheney and Bush," she said. "I'm a uniformed officer. I'd be in Leavenworth today if I signed my name to those kinds of things, the humorous, contemptuous statements."

Kwiatkowski retired in February 2003, a month before the Iraq war began, and now teaches high school biology. The summer after she retired, Seymour Hersh visited her and they spent hours talking about the Office of Special Plans. Kwiatkowski told me she did not believe she provided him the "cabal" quote that became ingrained as truth in the paranoid fantasies of the Left. But, she told me, "It's consistent with what I saw there. They saw themselves as the movers and shakers. A cabal."

Feith and other policymakers were aghast at Kwiatkowski's influence. Senator Edward Kennedy, a Senate Armed Services Committee member who likened U.S. troops to Saddam's butchers, appeared before the august Council on Foreign Relations. It was the first anniversary of the Iraq invasion. The Washington press corps lavished hours of coverage on the speech. Midway through his denunciation of the Bush administration and the war, Kennedy cited one Karen Kwiatkowski as a reliable source.

Said the senator, "Lieutenant Colonel Karen Kwiatkowski, a recently retired Air Force intelligence officer who served in the Pentagon during the buildup to the war, said, 'It wasn't intelligence—it was propaganda...they'd take a little bit of intelligence, cherry-pick it, make it sound much more exciting, usually by taking it out of context, usually by juxtaposition of two pieces of information that don't belong together.'"

In retirement, Kwiatkowski remained active in libertarian politics and journalism, writing for Internet outlets like LewRockwell.com (an antiwar libertarian site), MilitaryWeek.com, and the liberal huffingtonpost.com. For the liberal website Salon.com she wrote an article in March 2004 under the headline, "A high-ranking military officer reveals how Defense Department extremists suppressed information and twisted the truth to drive the country to war." That led to her being invited inside the secure confines of the Senate Intelligence Committee, which wanted her to provide the facts backing up her article's accusations. She could not.

Kwiatkowski told me she sat at a table surrounded by forty staffers. "There was nothing to drink. There were no breaks," she said of the three-hour session. When I asked her what specifically Luti's office did wrong, she said it helped write speeches for Bush and collected its own intelligence by interviewing Iraqi defectors at off-site hotel rooms. The Pentagon says this did not happen.

The Senate committee's bipartisan final report contained this sentence about Kwiatkowski: "The desk officer told committee staff that she believed there was a hostile environment between the Office of Special Plans and the DIA, but could not provide any examples of a hostile climate." (The one example she had mentioned had been the dispute over the word *assassination*, not pressure to change intelligence.) The committee report continued, "She had no direct knowledge to support any claims that intelligence analysts were pressured and much of what she said is contradicted by information from other interviews and intelligence reporting."

Kwiatkowski told me staffers never followed the leads she provided. "Stuff I was writing, that's mainstream now," she said.

MALOOF'S DEMISE

As Michael Maloof and David Wurmser completed their terror-linkage report in December 2001, Maloof suddenly found himself under attack from known and unknown adversaries. The known was Air Force lieutenant general Michael Hayden, who then ran the National Security Agency and would later become CIA director. Hayden accused Maloof of leaking classified material to the press and wanted his security clearance pulled—a death blow to a defense analyst. Without access to intelligence reports, it would be impossible to advise policymakers.

Maloof denied the allegation and subsequently passed a polygraph test. But as the process of stripping his clearance proceeded in 2002, newspaper articles began appearing about his case. Reporters quoted unnamed "intelligence sources" accusing Maloof of misdeeds. To Maloof, it was too much of a coincidence: he butts heads with Langley over acquiring years of reporting on al Qaeda, and a few months later his credibility is under attack from the intelligence community.

Maloof had courted controversy throughout his career. The congressional Cox Commission on Chinese spying and Rumsfeld's ballistic missile commission had loved his work. But CIA higher-ups found some of his contentions wrong-headed, such as his belief that the Lebanese Hezbollah, an arm of Iran, had played a role in the September 11 attacks. Maloof maintained contacts with Imad Hage, a Lebanese American discredited by the CIA who claimed to have special sources in Iraq, Syria, and Iran. "I received an urgent phone call tonight from Imad Hage," Maloof wrote in one e-mail to Feith's office. Hage claimed to have sources who told him Hezbollah planned attacks on high-level Defense Department personnel. (The Baghdad command later developed intelligence of Hezbollah's involvement in training Shi'ite insurgents to attack Americans.)

The DIA revoked Maloof's clearance in December 2001. Its order did not cite leaking. Instead, it said he showed a lack of judgment by getting into a romantic relationship with Ia Meurmishvili. The woman, a native of the Republic of Georgia, was being recruited by intelligence agencies. Maloof said the relationship began after he had separated from his wife. He later married Meurmishvili. The board also cited Maloof for unacceptable financial debt. Maloof said the debt crunch stemmed from his separation and divorce.

Feith came to Maloof's aid in October 2002, writing a memo to the DIA's Security Appeals Board (SAB), which can be found in the Appendix. "Sometime after his separation, he reported that he would be entering into a relationship with the Georgian foreign national, whom he has since married," Feith wrote. "Having known Michael for many years personally and professionally, I do not believe he would have allowed himself to be compromised in any way. On the issue of his personal affairs, including financial issues, he has undertaken a serious, documented effort to straighten them out." Feith cited Maloof's "patriotism and sense of duty and his commitment to security."

The memo worked. The appeals board voted a week later to reinstate his clearance. But the next spring, the board voted to revoke his clearance again, not on new charges, but on "the same information considered by the earlier SAB," stated a 2005 Pentagon inspector general's report.

Maloof lost subsequent appeals, and so Feith put him to work on unclassified projects. In 2004, Maloof paid a visit to Feith's Bethesda home. By then,

Senators Levin and Rockefeller had Feith clearly in the bull's-eye, accusing him of a rogue intelligence operation. The visit's agenda was to discuss the Senate investigation. Maloof started ticking off what his intelligence sources had been telling him, according to a memo he later wrote. Feith was stunned. Maloof's single-handed intelligence collection was just what Levin was complaining about. "Mr. Feith expressed growing irritation I was undertaking this effort and stated that it was all he could do to stop the public perception that I was setting up his office to give the appearance of running a rogue intelligence operation to bypass the intelligence community," Maloof wrote in a memo afterward. "Mr. Feith made it clear that he wanted my attempts to pass information to cease immediately." Discouraged, Maloof subsequently retired after more than twenty years of tracking arms proliferation between Western countries and the bad guys.

The intelligence community had bagged Maloof. Feith was damaged. Other targets awaited.

"When I drove out to the CIA, I thought we would be a team," Maloof recalled of his October 2001 trip to Langley. "As I tell people now, Rome was burning and the barbarians were at the gate. By October, it was open warfare. They began leaking and making accusations and accusing us of setting up an operation to bypass the agency. They went after me for political reasons." And they won.

TARGET: AHMED CHALABI

After Desert Storm failed to oust Saddam, President George H. W. Bush signed a secret order in the summer of 1992 authorizing the CIA to foment a coup in Baghdad. About that time, an Iraqi dissident, Ahmed Chalabi, traveled to a secure room in the basement of the Rayburn House Office Building. There he met with like-minded lawmakers who wanted Saddam gone. "We founded the mujahadeen," said Democratic congressman John Murtha, an ex-Marine who then believed in using American might, or proxies, to topple despots—and who would later turn against the war in Iraq. "And that is what we're going to do with you." However, Murtha's staff was less than forthcoming about the meeting. "Mr. Murtha does not recall such a meeting where he was present," said Matthew Mazonkey, the congressman's spokesman.

It was the beginning of Chalabi as a world figure, the face of opposition to one of the world's worst tyrants. The CIA built him up. And, like other figures the Agency came to see as threats, eventually tore him down via the tried-and-true method of the media leak.

A year after the Murtha encounter, Chalabi, with the CIA's help, founded the Iraqi National Congress (INC), an umbrella organization for anti-Saddam people dominated by Kurds and Shi'ites. The CIA, working through the INC, tried nine coups between 1991 and 1994. All failed.

The INC-CIA marriage broke up after a failed 1996 coup attempt. The CIA believed Chalabi withheld crucial information and maintained disturbing ties with Iran. Iran, a foe of Saddam's Sunni-dominated regime, was a safe haven for thousands of exiled Iraqi Shi'ites. But the CIA did not want information Chalabi gave the INC to leak to the fervently anti-American regime in Tehran.

Although the CIA now spurned him, Chalabi was far from finished. He had backers in Washington, especially in groups of conservatives who pushed the Clinton administration, and then the Bush administration, to target Saddam. Ironically, Chalabi, who became a target of Washington media and liberal Democrats after George W. Bush was elected president, had been resurrected by Clinton.

Clinton signed the Iraq Liberation Act of 1998 naming the INC as an official opposition group. The law paved the way for the Pentagon to support Chalabi. After the September 11 attacks, Chalabi went to the Pentagon at least four times to meet with top policymakers, including policy chief Douglas Feith.

The CIA watched in horror. Its experience with the exile in the 1990s told the Agency Chalabi was the wrong man to play any leadership role in Iraq. Joined by the State Department, the CIA launched a campaign to discredit Chalabi within the administration, with the American public, and with freedom-minded citizens in Iraq.

The CIA began spitting out a stream of analysis and field reports on Iraq. Virtually every one bashed Chalabi as an incompetent and a liar. Feith and his staff remarked that they had never seen such a concerted effort to destroy one man. They likened the Agency to a woman scorned, who spent the rest of her life getting even with her former lover. Feith came to believe the CIA wanted the president to hate Chalabi.

Officials referred to the INC and other Iraqi dissidents not as exiles but as "externals." That way, they captured not only the expatriates but also the Kurds in northern Iraq who opposed Saddam. Soon the CIA, supported by the State Department, issued papers railing against not only the INC, but also virtually every external group. The CIA favored Iyad Allawi, who had founded the Saddam-opposing Iraqi National Accord in 1990, two years before the creation of the INC.

Reporters told Feith that deputy defense secretary Richard Armitage was leaking against Chalabi, and also that State Department sources had told them the Pentagon had hand-picked Chalabi as the next leader of Iraq. Feith thought this was a deliberate lie. Rumsfeld had made it clear in dozens of pre-war meetings that the Iraqis would eventually elect their leaders. Working with Chalabi to oust Saddam did not mean helping him gain power for himself.

Armitage became a major background source for reporter Bob Woodward's third book on Bush, *State of Denial*, a critical portrait of the commander in chief, Rumsfeld, and Feith. Bush had sat down with Woodward for his first two books, but declined to do so for the third. People interviewed by

Woodward had told the White House the book would be uncomplimentary. *State of Denial*, like Woodward's other books, was a big bestseller, containing an exclusive inside look at crucial White House meetings.

Anonymous State Department officials complained to reporters that the Pentagon was making policy on its own, rather going through the normal interagency process in which decision-makers met to hammer it out together. Feith saw the irony. Rumsfeld pressed his aides not to bash other agencies in leaks to the press. The defense secretary went out of his way to get along with CIA director Tenet: They met for lunch weekly if their schedules permitted. One-on-one, they settled sticky intelligence issues, such as where to position satellites to the military's best advantage. Federal law states that if the defense secretary and the CIA director cannot reach an agreement on intelligence assets, the president will settle the matter. But Tenet and Rumsfeld were always able to work it out between themselves.

Meanwhile, the CIA and State Department bureaucracies, natural allies for years, leaked constantly against the Pentagon, and then blamed the Pentagon for a breakdown in the process. Rumsfeld told a probing Woodward, "You also know that I'm not the kind of guy who's going to say bad things about my colleagues. I just don't do it."

For his part, Feith says he maintained an open-door management style. When a topic emerged for discussion, he encouraged policymakers to brief him, accompanied by as many subject experts as wanted to come. A frequent topic was the CIA's war on Chalabi. Feith and others at the Pentagon viewed the CIA campaign against Chalabi as extremely damaging to Bush. The leaks to the press sent a message that the United States was about to hand-pick the next leader of Iraq. In 2007, while doing research for a book after he left the Pentagon, Feith searched for any Defense Department memo that promoted Chalabi as the next Iraqi prime minister. He found none.

The State Department's behind-the-scenes war on Feith went public in 2005. Retired Army colonel Lawrence Wilkerson, Secretary of State Colin Powell's chief of staff, said of Feith in *GQ* magazine, "Seldom in my life have I met a dumber man." Feith was perplexed, as he had never met Wilkerson. Wilkerson also said that at one interagency meeting, Feith stood up and screamed. Feith could not recall Wilkerson ever attending a National Security Council meeting.

All the while, the press repeatedly reminded the public that a Jordanian court charged had Chalabi in 1992 with embezzling funds. Chalabi had co-founded the Petra bank in Jordan in 1977 and had become rich. In 1989, as the bank collapsed under the weight of faulty transactions totaling $200 million, Chalabi moved to London, where he lived in comfort.

What was not reported was this: Jordan's ruler at the time, King Hussein, while friendly with the U.S. and Israel, was also a strong supporter of Saddam Hussein and vehemently opposed U.S. intervention to liberate Kuwait. Chalabi stood as Saddam's most prominent opponent in exile. The charges were brought by a military court controlled by the king.

CHALABI'S RETURN

With the invasion near, Chalabi traveled to the relative safety of Kurdish Iraq, waiting for Baghdad to fall. When the invasion was launched in southern Iraq, American forces were surprised to find that some Shi'ites, who were supposed to welcome them as liberators, instead protested the invasion. An office at the Pentagon phoned Chalabi's contingent for help. Soon, six military planes were flying more than six hundred Chalabi supporters into southern Iraq to soothe emotions. This account dispels a media myth that Chalabi's entrance was an orchestrated grand arrival, a prelude to Chalabi being the next ruler of Iraq. Rather, he was used as an intermediary to the Shi'ites. When the United States put together the first interim government, it was CIA favorite Iyad Allawi, not Chalabi, who headed it. Chalabi lacked a strong domestic base of political support and did not do well in elections, perhaps because he was too secular for the Shi'ite majority. His dream of running Iraq was over.

The press attacks in Washington heated up in that first year of Iraq liberation. Chalabi, said unnamed intelligence officials, had tricked the U.S. into going to war. He had provided defectors who told the CIA lies about Iraq's weapons of mass destruction. An unnamed former CIA officer who was involved in Middle East spying started popping up in press reports bashing Chalabi and Douglas Feith's policy shop. Some press reports said Chalabi profited from the UN oil-for-food bribery scandal. In Iraq, Chalabi began railing against the occupation leadership of Paul Bremer and his Coalition Provisional Authority. Chalabi demanded elections now, not later. "My relationship with the CPA now is nonexistent," he declared.

One night in April 2004, Francis Brooke, a close political advisor of Chalabi's, received a call from Larry Franklin, a Pentagon aide who had helped Chalabi arrange prewar meetings at the Pentagon. By that time, Franklin was being investigated by the FBI for sharing classified information with workers at the American Israel Public Affairs Committee (AIPAC) about Iran's devious activities in Iraq. On that night, months before he would plead guilty in court, Franklin was cooperating with the government. FBI agents were trying to prove that Chalabi had shared sensitive U.S. code-breaking information with Iran, so they turned to Franklin, who then turned to Brooke. Brooke shared the conversation with me, saying that he remembers it vividly because it was so bizarre. Franklin's attorney would not return my calls about it.

"You've got a real problem with the Iranian intelligence story out there and I can help you spin the press, if you tell me what really happened," Franklin told Brooke, his voice agitated.

"Larry, nothing happened. It's all bullshit," Brooke responded.

Growing angry, Franklin said, "You have to take this seriously."

"I'm not going to take it seriously," Brooke said. "I'm not going to worry about it."

The press, however, did take it seriously; they went wild over Chalabi's alleged sharing of America's top code-breaking secrets with Iran, and most reports simply assumed that he was guilty and treated the allegations as fact. Stories quoted "intelligence sources" as saying Chalabi had learned about U.S. code-breaking from a drunken service member and had notified Iran. The *New York Times* reported that FBI agents had given lie detector tests to key Feith aides. I spoke with Feith and five members of his senior staff. None said they had been given polygraphs by the FBI. None knew of any aide who had been targeted for such tests.

Chalabi was in Najaf, Iraq, at the time, trying to broker a cease-fire between U.S. forces and radical Shi'ite cleric Muqtada al-Sadr. His aides said he was the victim of a CIA campaign to destroy him. Chalabi said it was "false" and "stupid" to assert he had tipped Iran to the code-breaking. "Where would I get this from?" he said. "I have no such information. How would I know anything about that? That's stupid from every aspect."

The FBI probe, whatever its dimensions, did not stop Chalabi from returning to the United States in November 2005 as Iraq's deputy prime minister. In good graces again, Chalabi met with Secretary of State Condoleezza Rice, Vice President Cheney, and other senior officials and testified to the Senate Intelligence Committee on prewar intelligence.

By then, Democrats had settled on a media strategy: paint Chalabi as a liar and a spy who took America to war with phony evidence provided by INC-sponsored defectors. This provided an angle of attack on the Republicans. Democratic senator Richard Durbin of Illinois called the 2005 meetings between Chalabi, Rice, and Cheney "totally inappropriate." "How can you have the Federal Bureau of Investigation say that he is under active investigation as to whether or not he leaked sensitive data to the Iranians, that could have endangered American soldiers, and this man is being treated like some visiting dignitary?" asked Durbin.

But Chalabi did not act like a man about to be charged with spying against the United States. Nor did Cheney, Rice, or the other officials he met act as if they were in the presence of a man who had given secrets to Iran.

Francis Brooke told me neither he nor Chalabi has ever been interviewed by the FBI. "It wasn't true," Brooke said. "We never had access to U.S. intelligence. Dr. Chalabi is a foreign national. I'm just a regular citizen and I have never had a security clearance. I never worked on any classified projects. I've never seen classified material in my life. I think you would have to look for some sort of political motive for that."

An administration insider told me the whole affair was based on an intercepted communication, the validity of which was never confirmed.

Chalabi lost at the ballot box, but he did not abandon his native country. He stayed committed to democracy, working from his home base in the Sunni-dominated Mansour neighborhood of Baghdad. In 2007, he headed the Popular Committee in an attempt to bring Sunni-Shi'ite peace and continued to work on a commission that identified the worst Ba'athist leaders under Saddam. Supporters point out that Chalabi's Iraqi National Congress stayed loyal to the goals it had stated before the war.

THE HAGEL-SNOWE EFFECT

In 2005 Senator Pat Roberts fought his final battle with Jay Rockefeller over Ahmed Chalabi and his INC. That year, as Chalabi eased back into the Washington fold, the Senate Intelligence Committee opened a separate probe into press reports that he and the INC had tricked America. The story was that Chalabi produced Iraqi defectors who told lies about Iraq's WMD, and those lies found their way into the most critical intelligence reports on which Bush had justified the war.

The committee staff found something quite different. But the final conclusions were examples, again, of a once bipartisan committee becoming overtly political just in time for the November congressional elections.

The INC had sponsored or referred at least thirty-three defectors before the war. Defectors, by nature, are dubious sources. Often their motives are money and a new life away from an oppressive regime. The committee staff pored over intelligence reports on what each defector told the CIA and DIA. It found a mixed bag. Some the CIA had dubbed fabricators. Others had coughed up useful information about Iraq's military strength.

In some cases, CIA intelligence reports exaggerated what a source said. One defector, described as "source one" in the report, told of Iraqi engineers with weapons-related experience going to work at certain facilities. In its reports, the CIA stretched his account to conclude that he had identified facilities as actual nuclear sites, when he had not. In 2004, a CIA report attempted to correct the record. It said source one "did not, repeat not, claim that any facility produced or worked on chemical, biological, or nuclear weapons. Those WMD connections were made by analysts and at times DIA officers writing and disseminating the reporting."

The DIA told the committee its experience with INC sources "is similar to that with many HUMINT sources. . . . INC sources in some cases provided verified and useful information that directly supported contingency planning and operations for Operation Iraqi Freedom. In other instances, the information was vague, incorrect or unverifiable." In the end, INC defectors prompted a series of instant intelligence reports, but only one made it into the 2002 National Intelligence Estimate on Iraq in a minor way.

The staff then prepared conclusions to reflect this. But when the committee convened in 2006 to approve them, Rockefeller had another plan. He also had the votes for a raw political move. He proposed a replacement conclusion that said INC sources were used to "support key intelligence community assessments on Iraq," and that their testimony was "widely circulated."

Republicans found this sentence ridiculous. Virtually all reporting on sources is widely distributed via the community's SIPRNet computer network. The defectors were not used to support key findings, and only one report had found its way into a minor part of the 2002 Iraq NIE. The bipartisan Robb-Silberman commission had agreed with these findings, writing that INC sources had "a minimal impact on prewar assessments."

Rockefeller then moved to strike a second conclusion and replace it with one that said the INC "attempted to influence United States policy on Iraq by providing false information through defectors directed at convincing the United States that Iraq possessed weapons of mass destruction and had links to terrorists."

Most committee Republicans, senators and staff, sat stunned. Rockefeller's conclusions were not justified by the investigation and the resulting report. It was as if the committee were producing two separate reports: the investigative part, and then the conclusion part based more on dubious press reports than on actual evidence. Rockefeller replaced four other conclusions in the report with more damning ones. When the vote came, two Republicans defected to vote with the Democrats: Senators Chuck Hagel and Olympia Snowe. Without them, Rockefeller's rewriting of history would have failed. The roll call underscored that Pat Roberts never had complete control of his own committee.

Roberts joined the other losing Republicans in writing a strong dissent. "The adopted conclusions are not supported by fact," they wrote. "Information supplied by the INC played only a minor role in the intelligence community's prewar judgments concerning Iraq's WMD programs or links to terrorism."

Rockefeller had removed a finding that stated, "INC information was not widely used by the intelligence community and played little role in the intelligence community's judgments about Iraq's WMD programs and links to terrorism."

Rockefeller's conclusion bashed INC defectors for falsely claiming that non-Iraqi Arabs trained at a complex called Salman Pak. But the Iraq Survey Group, the team sent into Iraq to investigate Saddam's regime, had concluded in 2005 that the Iraqi Intelligence Service "trained Iraqis, Palestinians, Syrians, Yemeni, Lebanese, Egyptian, and Sudanese operatives in counterterrorism, explosives, marksmanship, and foreign operations at its facilities at Salman Pak."

In the end, Francis Brooke, the Chalabi advisor, told me, "The problem was the CIA had no agents in Iraq. They had no human intelligence at all."

And so when it came to lay blame for its failures, the CIA chose to blame Chalabi.

SADDAM AND AL QAEDA

In September 2006 the Democrats on the Senate Intelligence Committee steered through another report to their liking. This one compared prewar reporting on al Qaeda's connection to Iraq with what was actually found in Iraq. The report was not good news for Feith and his work on terror connections. Sifting through the prewar reports of supposed contacts between Saddam's regime and al Qaeda, the committee said the intelligence community could confirm only one.

This confirmed the Left's charges that the Bush administration hyped inaccurate intelligence reports to justify war. The Right viewed the report as terribly flawed. It accepted the word of Saddam's incarcerated lieutenants, whose regime was built on lies. It ignored Saddam's frequent calls for jihad against America and his hosting of a conference of Islamic radicals. It did not include seized documents showing that the Fedayeen, Saddam's Gestapo-like security force, trained hundreds of foreigners in terror tactics.

The committee ignored the Iraqi Perspectives Project (IPP) produced by U.S. Forces Command in 2005. It pointed out that the Fedayeen, led by Saddam's son Uday and originally created in 1994 to crush dissenters, had become a terrorist training unit. It had trained hundreds of non-Iraqi Arabs in all sorts of terror tactics in the 1990s, according to its own diaries and memos seized after the invasion. The IPP called the Fedayeen's record-keeping "meticulous."

The U.S. Forces Command report said, "The Fedayeen also took part in the regime's terror operations, which they conducted inside Iraq, and at least planned for attacks in some Western cities. In documents dated May 1999, Uday Hussein ordered preparation for 'special operations, assassinations and bombings for the centers and traitor symbols in London, Iran and the self-ruled areas [Kurdistan].'"

Critics of the Intelligence Committee's report also asked what why it ignored Iraq's link to terrorist Abu Nidal. He was one of the world's worst pre–al Qaeda terrorists, whose operatives conducted more than ninety attacks in the Middle East and Europe, killing more than three hundred people. Where did he enjoy safe haven for years? In Saddam Hussein's Iraq—until gunmen killed him in August 2002, as President Bush was making the case for war.

Also enjoying Saddam's hospitality was Abu Abbas, leader of the Palestine Liberation Front and murderer of U.S. tourist Leon Klinghoffer aboard the Italian cruise ship *Achille Lauro* in 1985. U.S. forces captured Abbas in 2003 as he attempted to flee to Syria. He died of natural causes while in custody in 2004.

In addition, the U.S. knows that Iraqi intelligence operatives destroyed thousands of pages of Ba'athist regime documents as the invasion approached, and even as Americans stormed through Baghdad. What's more, satellite images captured hundreds of trucks lined up at the Syrian border as the attack loomed. The U.S. is still not sure what was in them. But whatever the cargo, it was important enough for members of Iraq's intelligence service, the fearsome Mukhabarat, to travel to border crossings, dismiss the guards, and control the procession themselves.

"One contact. That's not true. It's absolutely not true," Michael Maloof told me, referring to the Senate Intelligence Committee's assertion that intelligence reports confirmed only one contact shared by Iraq and al Qaeda. He said the report failed to touch on Iran, which harbored al Qaeda operatives, including members of bin Laden's family. CIA analysts contend that Shi'ites and the Sunni-run al Qaeda do not cooperate. The CIA is wrong, Maloof said. "There is a history of cooperation between Tehran and al Qaeda. When we pointed out they were cooperating, the Agency blew a gasket."

Said Douglas Feith, "Who turned out to be right? The Ba'athists and jihadists are allies every day fighting us in Iraq, so I think we turned out to be right."

The Senate report quoted captured Saddam aides as saying they had no relationship with the terrorist Abu Musab al-Zarqawi, the eventual leader of al Qaeda in Iraq, even though al-Zarqawi was in Iraq before the March 2003 invasion (a visit cited by Bush as proof of al Qaeda's ties with Iraq). But critics asked why regime figures would admit to any relationship with a serial killer targeting Americans. Al-Zarqawi had been in Iraq in 2002 and quickly forged relationships with prominent Iraqi Sunnis when he returned in 2003. This seemed to indicate, at a minimum, that Saddam's regime had allowed him to use Iraq as a safe haven as he recovered from wounds suffered in Afghanistan, and that they considered him an anti-American fellow traveler.

Nevertheless, one Senate Republican told me that critics on the right had overreacted. The report did not say no other contacts occurred. It said that at this point it could not confirm them. But in the media, and therefore in the court of public opinion, the report became a political tool of the Democrats, who took control of the Senate in the elections two months later.

Pat Roberts chose not to remain vice chairman of the Senate Intelligence Committee. He later remarked in private that his biggest regret was that Walter Pincus, the *Washington Post*'s crack intelligence reporter, never telephoned him for an interview. Aides found this a bit naive. The newspaper had plenty of Democrats and CIA moles as sources. The *Post*, which devoted a good amount of its Washington coverage to dissecting and investigating Republicans, did not need them as sources. The straightforward Kansas senator never fully understood why Democrats and their media allies were less interested in an objective discussion of intelligence than of its political implications.

Other important aspects of the Iraq intelligence failures were missed as well. Few if any reporters conceded that Stalinist states like Iraq, with layers and layers of security, are difficult to penetrate. Once Saddam Hussein was ousted, American intelligence gained unprecedented access to sources: they could comb through documents, visit military and weapons sites, and interview former regime officials. So it was a given that final, after-the-fact reporting on Iraq would be different from—and better than—intelligence based on a few unreliable defectors and satellite imagery. That does not mean that prewar intelligence was "cooked."

Regarding "pressure," of course, after the September 11 attacks policymakers pressured CIA analysts to come up with more information. The country was at war, and we did not know when or whence the next attack might come. The Bush administration desperately needed answers as quickly as possible about al Qaeda. It also needed to know whether Saddam Hussein, a ruthless dictator with a grudge against America, who was regularly firing on our planes patrolling Iraq's no-fly zones and who was refusing to cooperate with UN weapons inspectors (in violation of more than seventeen UN National Security Council Resolutions), might be in the terrorist mix.

LEVIN WINS

The Intelligence Committee staff had not found anything wrong with Feith's challenging of the CIA's analysis of al Qaeda's links to Iraq—so Levin, Rockefeller, and the CIA had to find another way to nail him.

Levin turned to the Pentagon inspector general. He took a special interest in the internal watchdog, headquartered across the Pentagon's sprawling parking lot in Pentagon City. Levin knew a report from the inspector general, structured the way he wanted it, was a powerful political weapon. His staff maintained good sources inside the bureaucracy.

Levin sent a letter to the inspector general demanding yet another probe of Feith's people. His letter even listed the ten questions the inspector should ask and set the parameters for what should be investigated. As the inspector general plowed ahead, Levin ascended to the Senate Armed Services Committee chairmanship. It is not uncommon for investigators to want to please their masters, in this case Levin and his newly empowered Democratic senators.

In February 2007, the inspector general submitted an unclassified report to Levin. It found nothing illegal or unauthorized in what Feith did in critiquing CIA reports on Saddam-terror links. Rockefeller's and Levin's repeated charges were unfounded. But the report did give the senators part of what they wanted. Acting inspector general Thomas Gimble wrote, "While such actions were not illegal or unauthorized, the actions were, in our opinion, inappropriate given that the intelligence assessments were intelligence products and did not clearly show the variance with the consensus of the intelligence community."

To be accurate, Feith's final analysis had not been much different from Tenet's assessment, which the CIA director had put in writing in a letter to the intelligence committee in 2002. Tenet said he did not rely on the Pentagon's work. "We have solid reporting of senior-level contacts between Iraq and al Qaeda going back a decade," Tenet told the committee. "Credible information indicates that Iraq and al Qaeda have discussed safe haven and reciprocal nonaggression. Since Operation Enduring Freedom, we have solid evidence of the presence in Iraq of al Qaeda members, including some that have been in Baghdad."

It should also be noted that Bill Clinton, not George W. Bush, was the first president to draw a link between Saddam's regime and al Qaeda, and to jus-

tify military action based on that connection. After al Qaeda bombers struck
two U.S. embassies in East Africa in 1998, Clinton retaliated by ordering
cruise missile hits on an al Qaeda camp in Afghanistan and on the al-Shifa
pharmaceutical plant in Sudan. The administration said the al-Shifa plant
produced components of deadly VX nerve gas, that bin Laden owned a stake
in the company, and that its manager traveled to Baghdad to learn bomb-
making techniques from Saddam's scientists.

William Cohen, Clinton's defense secretary at the time, elaborated when
he appeared before the 9-11 Commission in 2005. He testified that "bin
Laden had been living [at the plant], that he had, in fact, money that he had
put into this military industrial corporation, that the owner of the plant had
traveled to Baghdad to meet with the father of the VX program."

He speculated on the public's reaction if VX gas from that plant was used
to kill Americans. "'You had a manager that went to Baghdad; you had
Osama bin Laden, who had funded, at least the corporation; and you had
traces of [VX precursor] and you did what? And you did nothing?' Is that a
responsible activity on the part of the secretary of defense?"

Feith, now teaching at Georgetown University, celebrated his legal vindi-
cation and accused Rockefeller and Levin of unfounded "smears." He set up
a website to counter Levin's charges. He then went on a one-man media blitz
to denounce the inspector general's criticism of him for "inappropriate"
behavior. Under the inspector general's rules, Feith argued, CIA analysts
could never be challenged by a policymaker's different views. "It's healthy to
criticize the CIA's intelligence," Feith said on *FOX News Sunday*. "What the
people in the Pentagon were doing was right. It was good government."

Feith told me, "I think Levin has grossly distorted what the IG [inspector
general] said. The IG made an extremely technical point. Levin turned that
into 'the president lied to get us into war.' He blew the thing up a thousand
times bigger than what the IG actually said."

Challenging the CIA is what had started the Langley-Pentagon war in the first place. The Agency cringed at outside criticism. In the end, it won. Some of Bush's national security team had stopped getting their daily CIA briefings, or took them in writing, to avoid the possibility of leaks to the media or becoming the target of a Democrat-ordered probe. Now the inspector general had set legal precedent. To challenge a CIA product with an alternative view was "inappropriate." If you dared to do otherwise, you risked an investigation by the inspector general and accusations of criminality.

Vice President Cheney was a victim of CIA leaks that said he visited Langley to put political pressure on analysts. He was swayed neither by the Senate Intelligence Committee report (as amended by Rockefeller) on the links between Saddam and al Qaeda nor by the inspector general's report that said Feith's work had been inappropriate.

Cheney is a voracious reader of intelligence reports. In April 2007, when he went on Rush Limbaugh's radio show to hit Democrats for failing to send the president a "clean" spending bill for the Iraq war, he reminded Limbaugh's listeners of some neglected facts.

"Remember," said Cheney, "Abu Musab al-Zarqawi, a Jordanian terrorist, an al Qaeda affiliate. He ran a training camp in Afghanistan for al Qaeda, then migrated after we went into Afghanistan and shut 'em down there; he went to Baghdad. He took up residence there before we ever launched into Iraq, organized the al Qaeda operation inside Iraq before we even arrived on the scene, and then of course led the charge for Iraq until we killed him last June."

Al Qaeda has said that today Iraq is its main battlefront. Cheney believes that a loss to al Qaeda in the Iraq war would spur greater terror worldwide. He believes that Iraq was linked to al Qaeda before the war, and he knows al Qaeda is a leading factor in the insurgency now. Cheney wants to beat al Qaeda in Iraq. The Democrats want to convict the Republicans of using faulty intelligence to fight the Iraq war. And the CIA, for its own political interests, has been on the side of the Democrats.

CHAPTER 3

WAR ON THE WHITE HOUSE

"We've had a lot of leaks. . . . I don't know where they're from. Therefore, I'm not going to speculate. It turns out, you never can find the leaker. . . . That's an advantage you have in doing your job. . . . It would be helpful, if we can find somebody inside our government who is leaking materials clearly against the law, that they be held to account. Perhaps the best way to make sure people don't leak classified documents is that there be a consequence for doing so."

President George W. Bush, December 20, 2006, press conference

I t was a meeting so secret that some who attended vowed they would never acknowledge it ever happened. The ground rules mimicked the intelligence community's "plausible denial." Things are done in such a way that a president can deny he knew anything about it. In December 2005, the White House made one last attempt to convince the *New York Times* not to publish a certain story. The planned article would reveal one of the most secret intelligence programs in existence. The aim of this program was to prevent al Qaeda from attacking America. Shortly after September 11, 2001, President Bush, in one of his first significant acts in the war on al Qaeda, had signed a top-secret authorization. The authorization permitted the National Security Agency to begin monitoring communications from suspected al Qaeda operatives to people inside the United States.

The significance of Bush's order was that the NSA did not need to have a warrant for this surveillance. The NSA, the Justice Department, and President Bush would later justify the snoop-on-demand as crucial capturing of phone calls or e-mails on the spot. There was no time to first go before the Foreign Intelligence Surveillance Court (FISC), a secret Washington court created by the Foreign Intelligence Surveillance Act of 1978 that approved counter-espionage and counter-terrorism wiretaps. The Clinton administration had also bypassed the FISC by tapping the phones of American turncoat Aldrich Ames. Ames was a Soviet mole inside the CIA who went undetected for years despite plenty of clues to his treachery. It was another CIA counter-espionage failure. Bush aides maintained that the terrorist surveillance program was working so far. But now the *New York Times* planned to disclose it—on the grounds that the administration was breaking the law.

The pleas from the White House were not working with the editors at the *Times*. As a last-ditch effort, the administration convinced the four leaders of Congress's two intelligence committees—Senators Pat Roberts and Jay Rockefeller and Representatives Pete Hoekstra and Jane Harman—to meet with the paper's Washington bureau editors. It was an off-the-books meeting, intended never to be revealed, because the Bush team direly needed to prevent any leak about what it considered a major weapon in its anti-terrorist arsenal.

The Bush administration was much more diligent about preventing security leaks than previous administrations had been. When the administration briefed the four congressional committee members—not just on this program but, as oversight law required, on any extremely sensitive program—it demanded that only those four be present, without any staff. Congressional staffers were not used to being excluded. But when Roberts and Rockefeller went to the White House to be briefed on some covert operation, the White House specifically excluded staff director Bill Duhnke for the Republicans and Christopher Mellon for the Democrats. What's more, the Bush team prohibited the lawmakers from taking notes, as the CIA director and Vice President Cheney conducted the briefing themselves. It was a sharp departure from previous practice. Mellon worried about the White House's motivation for such secrecy. He worried that with no notes or witnesses, it would be Rockefeller's word against the White House's if any dispute arose. Mellon asked Rockefeller, "What's up?" after one secret meeting. Rockefeller simply smiled. "Can't tell you."

In December 2005, the big four presented themselves to the *Times*'s editors, willing to answer questions off the record. Had they been briefed periodically on the eavesdropping by the White House? Yes. Were there safeguards built in to protect civil liberties? Yes. Are you getting information that protects America? Yes. The four left the meeting thinking the *Times* might back off its scoop.

But just days later, much to the delight of the president's critics, the Sunday *New York Times* blared the news: "Bush Lets U.S. Spy on Callers Without Courts." The story stirred up the expected outrage at home, from groups like the American Civil Liberties Union, and abroad as well. Then, a double whammy. One of the story's writers published a book a few months later that disclosed the details of the warrantless surveillance. The book would have been printed at the time the intelligence committee heads met with the editors at the *Times*'s Washington bureau. People knowledgeable about the off-the-record meeting believe the *Times* snookered the big four. The editors knew they were going to run the story, because it was coming out anyway in the reporter's book. The meeting was nothing more than an effort to elicit more information on the program before the Sunday story went to press. The editors did not divulge that they planned to run the story; they listened as if there were a chance they might not run it. One of the four lawmakers later remarked privately there would be no more interviews for the *New York Times*.

Getting the NSA wiretap program into the media was the most prominent in the CIA bureaucrats' string of victories over the Bush White House. And in this case, the CIA's victim was the cause of American intelligence.

TIPPING OUR HAND

The real damage was more severe than an ethical betrayal of Roberts, Rockefeller, Hoekstra, and Harman. Al Qaeda already knew that American intelligence could intercept cell and satellite calls. But thanks to the *Times* story, and the reporter's book, it now knew much more. It knew American intelligence was targeting a particular type of call. If an al Qaeda operative punched cell phone numbers for someone in America, chances were he would be monitored. Several intelligence sources told me that al Qaeda radically changed its communications methods after the *Times* story. It found new ways to make contacts in the United States that NSA receivers couldn't intercept.

Congressman Pete Hoekstra of the House Intelligence Committee told me this:

> What happens is we have tremendous capabilities. Whenever you get one of these leaks...a capability we had is now international news.... You then immediately lose the special capability that you have because people are now aware of it.
>
> But what it also does is force people to go and focus on communications.... Remember, the communications that are targeted are known al Qaeda or terrorist organizations. That was the criteria: known terrorist organizations or [known terrorist] individuals calling into the United States. That was it.... It doesn't involve U.S. citizens.... There's no issue there. You've got to believe that 99.9 percent of these terrorist calls coming into the United States [have] information that we want and that we need to keep America safe.

Al Qaeda operatives don't call into the United States just for the heck of it. And people in the United States who are talking to al Qaeda operatives are... what we would call people of interest in the United States.... The end result [of our spying program being exposed] is these people change the way they communicate.

After the *Times* story, Rockefeller quickly told the press he had opposed the program all along. He disclosed a handwritten July 2003 protest letter he had sent Dick Cheney days after the vice president had briefed him.

Hoekstra said he, Rockefeller, and then minority leader Nancy Pelosi attended several briefings. "My take on it is you went into this meeting and you were briefed and kind of a last question was always..., 'You want any more information?' Other than the supposedly, the letter that Rockefeller wrote to himself and put into his drawer, no one ever expressed any concerns about this program."

LEAKS

There was one issue about which Hoekstra consistently complained: leaks. He was one of the first to start warning the White House, and specifically the president, that rogue elements in the CIA and in the intelligence community were leaking secret information to embarrass Bush and scuttle his war. The list of leaks grew longer as the war labored on. CIA station chief reports appeared in newspapers just days after they were written. Right before the 2004 presidential election, a negative CIA report on Iraq surfaced. Days before the 2006 congressional elections, a National Intelligence Estimate (NIE) leaked out. According to press reports, the NIE said the Iraq war was spurring more terrorism. But the White House, arguing that only the most negative findings in the NIE were published, took the extraordinary step of declassifying most of the document to present a more balanced view.

Someone leaked information to the *Washington Post* about where the CIA was holding the most senior captured al Qaeda operatives, including

September 11 planner Khalid Sheikh Mohammed. The sites dotted newly democratic Eastern European nations eager to help the United States out of gratitude for America's pushing the Soviet Union into the ash heap of history. The problem, as reported by the *Post*, was that the European Union operates under the rule of law. You just can't hold people indefinitely.

The story stirred up an international firestorm from human rights groups. The CIA later fired an employee named Mary McCarthy in connection with the story, although she denied leaking the information.

It was this stream of leaks that prompted Hoekstra to ring the warning bell at the White House, warnings that culminated in a personal letter to the president.

Hoekstra also told me about an incident in which he believed the CIA had leaked merely to try to embarrass him. As a courtesy to a colleague, former congressman Curt Weldon, a Pennsylvania Republican, Hoekstra agreed to travel with him to Paris to meet an Iranian expatriate who was a foe of Tehran's Islamic regime. This man, whom Weldon called Ali, had become an intelligence source for Weldon. Ali supposedly knew all sorts of secrets about the Iranian regime, including its ties to al Qaeda. The intelligence community thought little of Ali's information. Still, Hoekstra thought it was worth checking out, and met Ali in the City of Light. As a courtesy, once there he checked in with the CIA's Paris station chief. To the best of Hoekstra's knowledge, only he, Weldon, and the CIA knew about the visit. Weeks later, however, stories showed up in the press alleging that Hoekstra had been on a junket, rather than what the congressman considered a fact-finding trip to question a source that Weldon believed had invaluable intelligence information. Hoekstra kept a wary eye on Langley after that.

He began warning the White House in 2003, sometimes on the telephone, sometimes in person. "One of the areas where the president was getting hammered is by leaks out of the Agency," the congressman said later. He remembered his message as, "It appears that you haven't recognized not everybody...in the intelligence community buys into what you guys are doing and that they are actively undercutting your agenda."

He added, "Most of those leaks had a political component to them intended to embarrass or put the president on the defensive." The Bush administration, he said, "recognized that the bureaucracy, in some cases, had been eating them alive.... I think they recognized they had rogue elements within the CIA that were actively undercutting their agenda."

FALSEHOODS

Another target of CIA leaks was the White House National Security Council staff. Here the CIA charges were so serious that, if true, they could have brought down the presidency.

Potentially most damaging was an allegation from a CIA analyst that, in a pre–State of the Union meeting with an NSC staffer, the analyst told him to remove this sentence: "The British government has learned that Saddam Hussein recently sought significant quantities of uranium from Africa." These later became known as the "sixteen words." Bush said them in his January 2003 State of the Union address. What the president said was, strictly speaking, true. British intelligence did believe this to be the case and stood behind the claim, and even the CIA gave the report some credibility, not officially backing away from it until that summer. Soon, however, stories began appeared citing anonymous CIA sources who said the White House had persisted in keeping the sixteen words while overruling CIA analysts who demanded their deletion. In fact, this was not true, as soon became apparent when the charges came out into the open.

In one case, Alan Foley, director of the CIA's Center for Weapons Intelligence, Nonproliferation, and Arms Control (WINPAC), testified before the Senate Intelligence Committee. Anonymous CIA sources had told the mainstream media that the Agency had asked Robert Joseph, an NSC staffer for nonproliferation (who later moved on to the State Department) to remove the words *Niger* and *five hundred tons* from the draft State of the Union address.

The allegation appeared in the press and numerous left-wing blogs in 2003. Joseph knew it was not true. Joseph told the NSC staff such a conversation never occurred. His name was being muddied by the CIA, and he suspected that Langley headquarters was behind it. When questioned by Senate Intelligence Committee staff, Alan Foley initially supported the charge. But to his credit, he went back and checked. He reviewed the draft and found that indeed those two words had never been in the speech in the first place.

In a second case, another CIA analyst targeted another NSC staffer. The analyst told the Intelligence Committee that during a discussion with the aide over a speech (he could not remember which one) he told him to remove any reference to Iraq and Africa. In response, the staffer told investigators such a conversation never occurred.

In the end, the Senate Intelligence Committee's bipartisan report in 2004 sided with the White House against the CIA: "When coordinating the State of the Union, no Central Intelligence Agency analysts or officials told the National Security Council to remove the 'sixteen words' or that there were concerns about the credibility of the Iraq-Niger uranium reporting. A CIA official's original testimony to the committee that he told an NSC official to remove the words 'Niger' and 'five hundred tons' from the speech is incorrect." In his memoir, George Tenet himself conceded that the CIA failed to warn the White House before Bush delivered the State of the Union speech.

But by that summer, the damage had been done, and the Bush administration itself had conceded that the "sixteen words" should not have been spoken, because there was insufficient evidence to support them. Nevertheless, the CIA leaks against the NSC and the White House were wrong, and were found to be wrong by the investigating intelligence committee. Yet this went largely unreported in the press. In fact, to this day, left-wing critics of Bush continue to cite the original press stories, and thus propound the myth that the CIA pushed for changes in the State of the Union but were rebuffed by a politically charged NSC staff.

TARGET: JOHN BOLTON

In May 2002, a few days after John Bolton delivered a tough speech at the Heritage Foundation on global weapons proliferation, his chief of staff, Fred Fleitz, received a call from someone at the CIA. Fleitz didn't know the caller, but he would soon know him all too well. The caller would help end his boss's diplomatic career.

The man on the phone was Fulton Armstrong, the top Latin American analyst on the National Intelligence Council (NIC). All sixteen intelligence agencies are represented on the NIC, which reports to the CIA director and produces papers that reflect the intelligence community's collective assessments. The 2002 National Intelligence Estimate on Iraq was an NIC product.

Armstrong was upset. Bolton, undersecretary of state for arms control and international security affairs, had included a line in his speech that Cuba was pursuing germ warfare capability. Armstrong claimed it was not true. Worse, he accused Bolton of failing to get the required clearance from the intelligence community before delivering the speech. It was a serious charge.

The heated exchange found Fleitz informing Armstrong that the speech had been cleared in a rather arduous process. Bolton had delivered a similar speech the year before in Geneva, absent any reference to Cuba. He wanted to include Fidel Castro's dictatorship in his next speech on WMD. Fleitz informed his boss that the subject was classified. They produced a draft speech and started the clearance process with the State Department's Bureau of Intelligence and Research (INR). An INR official made the highly unusual move of putting a note on it saying it was wrong and inserting his own language.

The draft then went to the CIA's WINPAC. The NIC analyst for weapons of mass destruction reviewed it. A key change was made: instead of saying

Cuba had an actual biological weapons program, as Bolton had suggested, the speech said it had a "development effort" in germ warfare.

None of that mattered to Armstrong, who had been the Clinton administration's Latin American expert on the National Security Council. He had not been consulted. He launched a campaign against the speech inside the intelligence community. In June, he went directly to the staff of Senator Christopher Dodd, a senior member of the Senate Foreign Relations Committee and one of Bush's harshest critics. Armstrong lodged a complaint that Bolton had delivered the speech without clearance. It was a tried-and-true CIA tactic: attack a Bush official via Democrats in Congress. Someone leaked it to the news media. Dodd's staff put the allegation in their arsenal for the next run-in with Bolton.

Bolton found himself caught in a thirty-year Washington debate on Cuba. Senator Dodd, and his ally Armstrong, like many liberals, wanted to normalize relations with Fidel Castro. Bolton, like most of the Bush administration, did not.

A few weeks after Bolton's Heritage speech, Dodd summoned a group of intelligence experts to a private Senate Foreign Relations Committee briefing. He let them know that public talk that Castro dabbled in poison did not help the move for normalization of relations with Cuba.

In June 2002, a Republican staffer briefed the State Department about Dodd's closed meeting via an e-mail to the staff of Otto Reich. Reich was assistant secretary of state for Western Hemisphere affairs. He already had felt Dodd's wrath. Like Bolton, Reich was a conservative and a foreign policy hard-liner. Cuban by birth, Reich had helped carry out Ronald Reagan's anti-Communist policies in Central America and later served as ambassador to Venezuela. Reich had two strikes against him as far as the Washington liberal establishment was concerned: he opposed Fidel and, during the Reagan administration, had argued for supporting the anti-Communist Contras in Nicaragua.

When Bush nominated him in 2001 to be assistant secretary of state, Dodd had denied him a confirmation hearing. Reich served initially as a recess appointment, then transferred to the National Security Council, and finally left government in 2004.

The e-mail to Reich's office said that during the closed meeting Fulton Armstrong had launched into a tirade against Bolton. "Armstrong engaged in innuendo indicating that normal security procedures had been circumvented to secure clearance for the speech," the message said. According to this e-mail, Armstrong had tried to "minimize" Castro's wrongdoing, to the point that his CIA team leader had to correct him.

"It was clear," the Republican's e-mail said, "that this comment and his earlier statements were intended to cast uncertainty and doubt on the carefully worded intelligence community conclusions and the integrity of the clearance process to clear Mr. Bolton's speech." This e-mail marked the first firm confirmation that Armstrong had lodged a false complaint against Bolton with powerful Democrats like Dodd. The allegation would surface three years later at a critical time in Bolton's career.

A month after Bolton's speech, Fred Fleitz convened a meeting at the State Department's INR conference room. Attending were representatives from most of the government's sixteen intelligence agencies, including Fulton Armstrong from the CIA. Fleitz wanted to discuss Ana Belen Montes, one of the worst spies in U.S. history. Montes had been the Defense Intelligence Agency's senior analyst on Cuba. She was also a spy for Fidel, feeding the Communist regime reams of U.S. secrets. Fleitz thought it was a good idea to go back over all the intelligence community's products that contained input from Montes, because they might be disinformation or provide clues to what she gave Castro.

Armstrong vehemently opposed the back-checking, saying such review was unnecessary. He had worked on the same assessments as Montes and was sure she did not distort them. Armstrong was the community's senior officer on Cuba (and he had actually told analysts from the CIA's Cuban section not to attend the meeting). Participants remember the meeting as intense and heated, with Fleitz accusing Armstrong of having leaked to the press the false allegation that Bolton's Heritage speech hadn't been properly cleared. Because of Armstrong's seniority, others in the room deferred to him. There was no back-checking.

As the DIA's senior person on Cuba, Montes had talked relatively regularly with Armstrong and policymakers on Latin America. One former Pentagon official remembers her as fairly typical of the intelligence community. She briefed along these lines: Fidel had wide popular support, he was not a threat to the United States, and the long-standing economic embargo should be lifted. In other words, she and Armstrong saw eye-to-eye.

"I think she was there not so much as an agent of influence but as a genuine spy, collecting information and probably recruiting others who I'll bet you anything are still there," a Pentagon official told me.

A year after Bolton's Heritage speech, the Senate Intelligence Committee began investigating why the CIA had gotten the intelligence wrong on Iraq's WMD and whether Bush's team had pressured analysts to change conclusions. The probe, as we've seen, found they had not. Because CIA elements were targeting Bolton, intelligence committee staffers included Bolton in their investigation. Though he had nothing to do with the intelligence on Iraq's WMD, he too stood accused of pressuring intelligence analysts. Fleitz got a draft of that section and was aghast: it reported only Fulton Armstrong's side of the story. Fleitz quickly wrote a response, which was included in the finished report.

In 2005, Bush nominated Bolton as the next United Nations ambassador. It was one of the foreign service's most prestigious diplomatic appointments. The post was a bully pulpit that the articulate, plain-speaking Bolton was well suited to fill. Democrats on the Senate Foreign Relations Committee, however, had no intention of letting the nomination go through.

Though Republicans still held the presumptive majority on the committee, Democratic staff took the lead in pre-confirmation questioning. Aides to
the Republican committee chairman, Senator Richard Lugar, seemed unin-
terested, so Democratic staffers set up a closed-door star chamber and summoned witnesses one at a time. They acted like senators as they questioned
members of the intelligence community to get dirt on Bolton.

Fred Fleitz was called in for two private sessions. Most of the questions
dealt with how Bolton cleared his WMD speech with the CIA. The Democratic staffers, led by Dodd's aide Janice O'Connell, grilled Fleitz in an effort
to make him concede that Bolton was not always diplomatic when dealing
with intelligence analysts.

"We can do this the easy way, or the hard way," she said to Fleitz at one
point when he objected to a question. "It's up to you."

Fleitz wondered when GOP staffers would jump in to defend him or
Bolton. They never did. After his testimony, Fleitz learned that O'Connell had
remarked, "He'll never get confirmed to any post." When the confirmation
hearings began, Democrats relied on Fulton Armstrong to deep-six Bolton.
Senators cautiously referred to Armstrong as "Mr. Smith," thinking his work
was covert. In fact, his name appeared on the National Intelligence Council
website.

Bolton had a response to Armstrong's charge. "When I heard that somehow [Armstrong] was saying he hadn't been involved in the clearance
process, as a member of the National Intelligence Council, I said I'd never
heard of this individual. I didn't know his name," he told the committee. "I
checked with the CIA and they said, indeed, they had cleared the speech with
the national intelligence officer for science and technology, who has cog-
nizance over biological warfare issues and therefore was the right
NIO[national intelligence officer] to clear."

In fact, the clearance issue did not matter to Democrats. It was merely a
pretext to cast doubt on Bolton, using a CIA employee who would impress

Republican senators. The object was to encourage them to wilt and scuttle Bolton, thus embarrassing the Bush administration.

In his testimony before the committee, Bolton said that Otto Reich and he had, on separate occasions, told the NIC director that they were displeased with Armstrong's work. "I had lost confidence in Mr. Smith [Armstrong]," Bolton testified. "What I said was that, in my dealings with him, his behavior was unprofessional and that I'd lost confidence in him and supported Mr. Reich."

"Confidence because he didn't agree with you?" Senator John Kerry asked him.

"No. Absolutely not, Senator. Confidence because he was claiming the process failed; that was inaccurate and untrue," Bolton answered.

Bolton's backers repeatedly referred to page 277 of the 2004 Senate report on pre–Iraq war intelligence. That page begins its reporting on Bolton's run-ins with State Department and CIA intelligence analysts. It confirms that his speech, indeed, had been cleared by the NIC.

Nonetheless, Armstrong's allegation became part of the Democrats' case to deny him the ambassadorship. As in the Douglas Feith affair, if a Bush official questioned the work of a CIA analyst, he or she risked a Democrat-inspired investigation.

Bush used a recess appointment to put John Bolton at the United Nations. Bolton resigned after the Democrats won the November 2006 elections, his chances for a permanent appointment dashed. He returned to a chair at the American Enterprise Institute (AEI) and began writing a book about it all.

Armstrong left his senior post at the NIC. The CIA sent him abroad as an analyst in the clandestine service. The Agency declined to make him available for an interview.

BOLTON'S VIEW

The American Enterprise Institute is a maze of small offices that house some of the conservative movement's biggest luminaries, like Bolton, Lynne

Cheney, Michael Ledeen, and Ben Wattenberg. In the spring of 2007, I found Bolton in his windowed office a few blocks from the White House. He had just finished a televised discussion at AEI on Bush's deal with North Korea to end its nuclear program. Bolton does not like any part of the agreement with the Stalinist regime. Kim Jong-il will take the money, fuel, and food the U.S. offers, and then cheat, the ambassador said.

But on that day, I wanted to talk to Bolton about his failed confirmation to the UN, a slap in the face for a man who, by most accounts, had performed well in the job.

"There was a deliberate effort by some of the opponents to find information that would be disqualifying and I think it was supported by leaks out of the bureaucracy from people with whom I had had policy disagreements and who were seeking payback," he told me.

Was one of those opponents Fulton Armstrong?

"I don't have any doubt—because of what I know about his performance elsewhere—that he was in regular contact with the Hill and that he was one of the sources. I don't doubt that at all."

Was it proper for a CIA analyst to spearhead a campaign against a senior political appointee?

"I think it's highly improper. If there is supposed to be a wall of separation between intelligence and policy, then his opposition to me," he said, surely violated it. "I'd never met the man. I'd never questioned any of his intelligence judgments." Bolton told me that Armstrong came after him because he was not involved in clearing Bolton's Heritage speech, though the speech had been properly cleared with the relevant bureaucrats. "That speech was fully cleared within the bureaucracy and this was just a bureaucratic snit-fit that he then carried through Dodd's office into the confirmation process. He's part of the pro-Castro wing of the intelligence community. He was out of control."

Are there rogue elements at Langley bent on opposing the president?

"I'm sure it's true and this to me was an example of that, because in a way much of the battle over my nomination was a surrogate for policy disagreements with the administration as a whole."

Was Dodd fair to you?

"No, of course not. This was a hatchet job that he's tried on other nominees that he thinks are too unfriendly to Castro. It's not like he's opposed to all conservatives. It's just a particular obsession with people he deems not nice to Castro."

And this seems to hold true for Castro's friends as well. During one Senate Committee hearing, Senator Dodd even scolded Secretary of State Condoleezza Rice for criticizing Hugo Chavez, the virulent anti-American leader of Venezuela who is not only a Castro ally, but who has also pledged his support to Iranian president Mahmoud Ahmadinejad. Chavez used a speech at the United Nations to refer to President Bush as Satan.

TARGET: DONALD RUMSFELD

In September 2006, retired Army general John Keane paid a visit to Donald Rumsfeld and General Peter Pace, chairman of the Joint Chiefs of Staff. The session was gloomy. Polls showed the Republicans losing control of Congress in the coming election, only two months away, because of one issue: Iraq. The latest crackdown in Baghdad had failed to reduce the violence. Public support for the war stood about as high as the president's job approval ratings: 35 percent.

General Keane knew that the postwar strategies that had been employed so far in Iraq had been terribly flawed. In the summer of 2006, he talked with former deputy secretary of defense Paul Wolfowitz, former House Speaker Newt Gingrich, and other people who could influence the administration. Soon he was invited to see Rumsfeld.

Keane, a beefy ex-paratrooper and Vietnam combat veteran, was a Rumsfeld supporter. The secretary had eyed him to succeed Eric Shinseki as Army chief of staff in 2003. But Keane bowed out for family reasons, retired as vice chief of staff, started a consulting business, and played advisor to the Pentagon, including to General David Petraeus, who would become the top officer in Iraq in 2007. When six retired generals called for Rumsfeld to resign, Keane was willing to go on the record defending his old boss.

The liberal press created a myth about Keane that badly damaged Rumsfeld. In April 2002, Keane's name appeared in the *Washington Post* as the general Rumsfeld had picked to succeed Shinseki. Shinseki and Rumsfeld did not get along. Rumsfeld found him unresponsive in meetings, unwilling to engage in a brisk back-and-forth on the Army's future. Shinseki chose not to attend senior executive meetings, sending Keane instead. For his part, Shinseki believed he already had the Army on a good transformation path. He had beaten back an effort in early 2001 by Rumsfeld's bean-counters to trim the active force. His resistance would prove beneficial a few months later when the U.S. went to war and needed every soldier it could find.

The news media said Keane's name had been leaked by a Machiavellian Rumsfeld in order to label Shinseki a lame duck. But there is no evidence Rumsfeld orchestrated the leak. In fact, he hated such behind-the-scenes maneuvering.

Larry Di Rita, one of Rumsfeld's closest aides, said the whole story was phony because Rumsfeld had not picked anyone at that point to succeed Shinseki. Candidates were still being evaluated; moreover, Rumsfeld hated speculation in the press over who would get which job.

"Any idea of 'let's do something clever, like let the name get out there, so people would not focus on the chief and start focusing on the vice chief,' would have been idiotic," Di Rita told me. "Whoever perpetrated it did not know the facts or Donald Rumsfeld. It was contrary to the disciplined, respectful, and systematic approach Rumsfeld takes toward personnel decisions. At its core, the *Post*'s Keane-for-Shinseki intrigue story was also inaccurate, because no decision had been made. It was Washington mischief-making at its worst and most destructive to everyone involved." An Army source told me that Keane was, in fact, offered the job. The source said Keane believes someone in the Pentagon leaked his name, not to diminish Shinseki, but to clear up speculation over who would win appointments to four-star combatant commander posts then up for grabs. All service chiefs are, in effect, lame ducks. They serve one four-year term, then retire or move to another four-star billet.

Rumsfeld's people believe they know the source of the leak: Stephen Herbits, a multimillionaire executive who came to the Pentagon as a consultant. His job had been to help assemble Rumsfeld's civilian staff. But he had a team of people working for him who wanted to weigh in on officer selection as well. Rumsfeld's aides believe the Herbits team favored Keane and circulated his name as a way to advance him.

Regardless of their messy past, Keane supported Rumsfeld, and in 2006 wanted to provide him with constructive advice. When Keane entered Rumsfeld's office on September 19, 2006, he got right to the point. "The strategy is failing," he said. "I believe we are in a crisis in terms of the level of violence and, if unchecked, we have the real possibility that civil war will break out and we won't have to debate whether it is a civil war or not. It will also likely lead to a failed state. We do not have much time to be able to act. We have a matter of months to do something about it."

Rumsfeld took copious notes throughout Keane's presentation. One of his questions betrayed the defense secretary's own doubts: "So it's not too late?"

"My judgment," replied Keane, "is we are not out of time. There remains one thing we can do that could give us some decisive results. We must use force to bring down the level of violence so that we can get a political solution." Keane began outlining what would become the "surge" strategy.

Rumsfeld was uncharacteristically quiet throughout the briefing, which lasted more than an hour. Keane focused on two significant failures. After the invasion in 2003, Lieutenant General Ricardo Sanchez had worked on setting up a government and killing insurgents. "But there was no plan to defeat the insurgency and secure the population," Keane said, no anti-insurgency campaign plan.

When General George Casey arrived as the first four-star general to run Iraq in 2004, he and General John Abizaid, chief of U.S. Central Command (CentCom), settled on what Keane called the "short war." The idea back then was to fight the insurgents while building up the Iraqi Security Forces, which would take over the job. But building the new Iraqi army was slow, and the enemy was getting larger, more deadly, and more complex.

"Absent from the military strategy was any notion to defeat the insurgency ourselves," Keane said. "That was a conscious decision. This discussion had been lost on people. People did not understand that military strategy did not have as a centerpiece the defeating of the insurgency. It left open the insurgency and they exploited it. They were destabilizing the country."

Rumsfeld made one of his few responses. He said Casey and Abizaid created the plan and he supported it. Rumsfeld always played the optimist. When the Defense Policy Board was pessimistic, the defense chief would fire back, listing his men's accomplishments. "Something was different about him this time," Keane said. "I sensed a general sense of resignation about him."

Keane said the Iraqis were not ready for democracy. The 2005 elections in Iraq masked what was really going on: an insurgency whose elements now numbered more than 100,000 people.

Keane then made his recommendation: put more soldiers in Baghdad. The U.S. would never win as long as the Iraqi population was not secure. Rumsfeld needed to build up the Army to more than 500,000 soldiers. The Army needed to send its best officers and non-commissioned officers to embed with Iraqi units and train them.

"They already are," Rumsfeld said.

"That's not the case," countered Keane, who had done his own investigation.

Rumsfeld, then in his sixth year as defense secretary, had more problems than Keane's private critique. General Abizaid, who as a Joint Staff director and deputy CentCom commander played a role in all war planning, admitted to the Senate Armed Services Committee that too few troops were deployed for post-Saddam Iraq. Several books, including my own *Rumsfeld's War*, documented the slapdash way in which Rumsfeld's men planned for peacekeeping; no one inside the inner circle planned for combating an organized, deadly insurgency. The results: too few troops, not enough armored vehicles, no plan for counter-insurgency once Baghdad fell, little thought about what would be done with hundreds of captured insurgents, and no comprehensive political roadmap. As Keane said, the command had no campaign plan—normally a linchpin of any war—for counter-insurgency operations.

Even under intense criticism, Rumsfeld remained his plucky self. In 2005, he summoned John McCain for a private lunch to discuss why the senator was blocking a number of Defense Department nominations. The face-to-face did not go well. Rumsfeld wondered aloud how McCain could hold up critically needed people in time of war. McCain, a big war backer, took it as an assault on his patriotism. McCain later said he had no confidence in Rumsfeld's leadership. On the campaign trail, he called him one of the worst defense secretaries ever.

A few weeks before the November 7 elections, Rumsfeld invited about twenty assistant and deputy assistant service secretaries for a meeting. These were the people who recommended policy and who handled personnel and procurement problems. They took their seats, on which were copies of a ten-page list of Rumsfeld-driven accomplishments. The list included: creating a new military command, Northern Command, to protect the homeland; expanding the reach of U.S. Special Operations Command; ridding the Army of clunky Cold War weapons and creating a brigade-centric force that could get to the fight quicker; and empowering military intelligence to rival the CIA in collection ability.

There was no set agenda for the meeting. Rumsfeld talked of "very difficult times" and asked everyone to stick with it. He said he wanted to do such meetings frequently, though this was the first most of them had attended. Each official introduced himself and described what he did, which was a strange thing to do six years into Rumsfeld's tenure. Then the meeting was over. As they filed out, Rumsfeld handed each a poster of Uncle Sam. *We are at War*, it read. *Are you doing all you can?*

At what would be Rumsfeld's last full-blown press conference, on October 26, 2006, the secretary of defense was combative. Rumsfeld unleashed another attack on the press for ignoring positive stories about Iraq. When reporters persisted in asking about a public disagreement between Bush and Iraqi prime minister Nouri al-Maliki, Rumsfeld said, "You ought to just back off, take a look at it. Relax."

Rumsfeld's disdain for the Washington press spilled out when discussing benchmarks for Iraq. "I wouldn't waste a lot of newsprint trying to find daylight between everybody on this, or try to find things that are wrong with it. . . . You can point with alarm and say, 'Oh my goodness, you didn't make it.' And you can have a front-page article and everyone will have a good time. And we'll say, 'That's right, you didn't make it.' And then the ones that we make earlier than we thought, we'll never see it on the front page."

On Capitol Hill, with the election less than two weeks away, Republicans wondered why Rumsfeld could not put away the sword and show a little contrition.

Rumsfeld later told friends he realized in the summer of 2006 that he had become the symbol for all that did not work in the war. He needed to go. He had offered his resignation twice before, but each time President Bush's loyal nature won out. He rejected the first, and the second, even when Rumsfeld thrust the letter back into his hand. But now the president realized that his Iraq policy needed a serious change of direction. The U.S. death toll approached three thousand. Only one-third of the American people still supported the war. The insurgency, far from being defeated, was getting stronger.

Bush and Rumsfeld often talked privately in the Oval Office. By late summer, the president knew Rumsfeld wanted to resign, but Bush believed that if he discharged him so close to the congressional elections it would look like a desperate political knifing. So the president decided to wait until after November 7. The White House's number-one candidate was Robert Gates, who had been a loyal national security aide to Bush's father. Gates had no ties to the Iraq war. He was happily running Texas A&M when the White House called. He gave a tentative yes the Sunday before the election.

That was all Gates could do, because Rumsfeld's future was still unsettled. President Bush had yet to make a final decision. Two Pentagon insiders told me that if the GOP had held Congress, Rumsfeld would have stayed on.

But the day after the Republicans' disastrous defeat, there was Rumsfeld at Bush's side at the White House announcing his resignation. "It's been quite a time," Rumsfeld said. "It recalls to mind the statement by Winston Churchill, something to the effect that 'I have benefited greatly from criticism, and at no time have I suffered a lack thereof.'"

Rumsfeld thought of himself in the mode of Churchill, a man vilified by the Left for his warnings on Nazism in the 1930s and who saw defeats in World War II eventually lead to victory.

In the Republican Party, the timing pleased few. Some wondered why, if Bush planned to oust Rumsfeld, he did not do it in time to announce a change of military strategy before the election, giving the party a better shot at holding Congress. Rumsfeld's backers complained that Bush had made their man a scapegoat for the GOP's electoral defeat.

I encountered ex-secretary Rumsfeld in February 2007 at a Hoover Institution reception in Washington. He was holding court as a steady stream of well-wishers lavished praise on him. I saw my opportunity and told him I was working on a story on his expansion of special operations. "Come by and I'll tell you how I did it," Rumsfeld said.

When I returned later to remind him of his commitment, he suddenly remembered a story I had written for my former employer, the *Washington Times*. To me, it was a fairly innocuous piece. There had been chatter in the Pentagon that Rumsfeld had remained on the payroll as he and a large staff ran a transition office and sorted thousands of pages of documents. I wrote a story that debunked those rumors. Rumsfeld, like other former secretaries, had a small transition staff. And he wasn't paid.

But Rumsfeld remembered it otherwise. "That was a terrible story you wrote. You of all people," he suddenly said, with rising anger. "I have never taken a dollar of government money improperly." I told him I had always tried to cover him fairly. "Horrible story," he shot back.

In that moment, I had experienced the "Rumsfeld dress-down" so many generals and civilian advisors had felt during his six-year tenure.

But if Rumsfeld remained as feisty as ever, there was no hiding the fact that the CIA had, again, seen the defeat of one of its rivals. Rumsfeld had challenged CIA analysts and built up the Pentagon's own intelligence capabilities. Now he was gone, and his replacement, Robert Gates, was a career CIA analyst who had complained in the *New York Times* about the Pentagon encroaching on Langley.

END OF AN ERA

A month after President Bush announced Rumsfeld's departure and Gates's arrival, the Iraq Study Group, a collection of "wise men" headed by former secretary of state James Baker and former congressman Lee Hamilton, released a list of recommendations. It called the situation in Iraq dire. It called for direct talks with Iran and Syria and a withdrawal of most American combat troops by early 2008. Bush, however, did not want to have direct talks with either Syria or Iran. Nor did he want to set a precise timeline for withdrawal, which he believed would tell the enemy that if they were patient, they would win.

But the study group had spurred Bush to order his own massive strategy review. Nearly every federal agency participated. The president wanted to hear directly from his own group of "wise men." So on December 10, 2006, he sat in the Oval Office and listened. In the room were three retired four-star generals, all Army: Barry McCaffrey, a persistent critic of Rumsfeld's management of the Army; Wayne Downing, Bush's first counter-terror chief at the White House until he lost a power struggle with Rumsfeld; and John Keane, who had given Rumsfeld his own frank assessment of the need for a new strategy.

"Hey, big guy, you're looking pretty good," the president said to Keane.

"Well, I have a life now," Keane joked, a reference to being freed from the Army's 24-7 work schedule.

Two think-tank types, Eliot Cohen and Stephen Biddle, sat on couches nearby, as did the president's most trusted advisors: Vice President Dick Cheney, Cheney aide John Hannah, press secretary Tony Snow, Karl Rove, John Bolton, and Stephen Hadley.

Downing wanted the military to send more special operations forces to train Iraqis. McCaffrey wanted a larger Army and was pessimistic about the prospects for stabilizing Iraq. Neither supported an escalation in troop strength.

When it was Keane's turn, he had about ten minutes to condense what he had told Rumsfeld two months ago. "There is still something we can do that is decisive," Keane said. The retired general then called for people to get fired. He said there had been no one held accountable for failures in Iraq. He did not mention General George Casey's name, but he was thinking of him. Casey's two offensives to recapture Baghdad that summer had both failed. Yet

Rumsfeld and Bush had rewarded him by naming him the next Army chief of staff.

Bush did not take sides, but listened and asked a few questions. A month later, on January 10, 2007, Bush told the nation of a new strategy for Iraq. He could have called it the "Keane Plan." The Army would grow. And he ordered more than 21,000 additional Marines and soldiers to Iraq. Commanding them would be General David Petraeus, who returned to Iraq in February. Gone was the old method of clearing a neighborhood and leaving. Now the sweeps would be followed by joint security stations and smaller combat posts permanently embedded in Baghdad's violent neighborhoods. Four years into the war, Keane finally saw the right strategy being employed. The question now was whether there was time for it to work.

CHAPTER 4

THE PR GAME

"The committee did not find any evidence that intelligence analysts changed their judgments as a result of political pressure, altered or produced intelligence products to conform with administration policy, or that anyone even attempted to coerce, influence or pressure analysts to do so."

Report of the bipartisan Senate Intelligence Committee on the 2002 National Intelligence Estimate on Iraq, July 9, 2004

"The intelligence community did not make or change any analytic judgments in response to political pressure to reach a particular conclusion, but the pervasive conventional wisdom that Saddam retained WMD affected the analytic process.... We have no found evidence to dispute that it was, as the analysts assert, their own independent judgment—flawed though they were—that led them to the conclusion that Iraq had active WMD programs."

Report of the bipartisan Robb-Silverman Commission on the Intelligence Capabilities of the United States Regarding Weapons of Mass Destruction, March 31, 2005

Paul Pillar was quite a catch for the staid School of Advanced International Studies (SAIS), an arm of Johns Hopkins's collegiate empire. Pillar was the CIA's national intelligence officer for the Near East and South Asia: the heart of the ideological and military battle against al Qaeda.

His region was, in fact, the war on terrorism. He had the opportunity to ana-lyze all sorts of reports on al Qaeda, and in 2003 agreed to talk to SAIS students and faculty about the war. But attendees at the private session got more than they'd bargained for. Pillar set out a scathing criticism of President Bush's "Axis of Evil" speech. It was wrong, he said, to link counter-terrorism and counter-weapons of mass destruction. They were two separate issues. In this speech, Pillar, a senior administration member, was thus opposing a central plank of the Bush administration's foreign policy. One alarmed listener took notes and later circulated them among Bush administration officials. It confirmed to them that they had another enemy at Langley.

The Bush team considered it unprofessional for a senior CIA executive to bash the president in public. The SAIS appearance was not the first time Pillar had criticized the administration's war policy. Washington columnist Robert Novak reported that Pillar had expressed his anti-administration leanings during a 2004 talk in California, in which he ridiculed the president's Middle East policies, especially concerning the deteriorating situation in Iraq.

Pillar was a senior director inside the CIA's Counterterrorism Center, the bin Laden watchers, in the late 1990s when al Qaeda grew and declared war. Yet he opposed military action as ineffective. "There were people at the senior level of the CIA who really opposed the administration," said an advisor to Langley. "One guy who particularly fit that was Paul Pillar. . . . Terrorism for them was just looked at as a hiccup and not as a major contingency."

Pillar decided to put his opposition to Bush in writing, taking leave from Langley to become a senior fellow at the liberal Brookings Institution. He wrote a book, *Terrorism and U.S. Foreign Policy*, which is viewed by conservatives as so out of step with the terror threat that at least one professor at a major university teaches the book as how *not* to think about al Qaeda.

For example, Pillar writes that it was highly unlikely al Qaeda could acquire weapons of mass destruction. He said it would be "a mistake to rede-

fine counter-terrorism as a task of dealing with catastrophic or super terrorism" because "these labels do not represent most of the terrorism that the
United States is likely to face."

But the subsequent invasion of Afghanistan showed that al Qaeda was, and
is, bent on obtaining horrible weapons. The 2005 bipartisan Robb-Silberman
Commission on the Intelligence Capabilities of the United States Regarding
Weapons of Mass Destruction said the picture the U.S. obtained from captured documents and debriefed terrorists "shed startling light on al Qaeda's
intentions and capabilities with regard to chemical, biological, radiological,
and nuclear weapons." Preemptive strikes against potential terror weapons
are a linchpin of Bush's counter-terrorism strategy. But Pillar writes, "The
overt preemptive use of military force against terrorists is unlikely and
unwise." He all but dismissed the benefits of precision strikes such as the ones
on Libya in 1986 and on Iraq and Afghanistan in 1998. "The terrorists'
response to a retaliatory strike may be counter-retaliation rather than good
behavior," said Pillar.

What galled the Bush administration most was Pillar's argument that
"Counterterrorism is a fight and a struggle, but it is not a campaign with a
beginning and an end. Perhaps a better analogy is the effort by public health
authorities to control communicable diseases. That effort, like counterterrorism, deals with threats that come in many different forms, some more virulent than others." He continues, "Even the abhorrence of terrorism that
touches U.S. interests directly should not lead the United States to reject
peacemaking with a group out of hand." Pillar even borrows from a 1960s
antiwar chant when he leads one part of the book with "Give peace a chance."
The Bush administration, on the other hand, sees al Qaeda and global terrorism as a threat that needs to be decisively defeated. The gap between Pillar and the administration was huge.

One intelligence advisor told me Pillar's writing helps explain why so
many at Langley opposed Bush's War on Terror. "Here was the guy in charge

of the Middle East division opposing just about everything Bush did," the advisor said.

When the Princeton-educated Pillar retired, he moved from bashing Bush in occasional speeches to becoming an open anti-Bush polemicist. He thus joined a number of other Langley alumni who, through books, articles, and media appearances, accuse Bush and his people of crimes and incompetence. Pillar's debut came in an article he wrote for *Foreign Affairs* magazine, in which he charged matter-of-factly that "the intelligence community's own work was politicized." He added, "The actual politicalization of intelligence occurs subtly and can take many forms." He wrote that CIA analysts had advised the White House to keep the famous "sixteen words" about Iraq looking for uranium in Niger out of the president's speech, when, in fact, the congressional inquiry showed they had not. He wrote that Feith's hard-charging policymakers created "a poisonous atmosphere" that "reinforced the disinclination within the intelligence community to challenge the consensus view about Iraqi WMD."

The problem with the article was that Pillar offered no proof. It was more feel than substance. There were neither internal memos nor even anonymous quotes from his colleagues at Langley to back up his assertions. More important, the two panels that exhaustively investigated the matter—the Senate Intelligence Committee and the bipartisan Robb-Silberman commission— found no such evidence. Pillar the essayist also seemed to disagree with Pillar the national intelligence officer. The commission report quoted him as saying about the 2002 Iraq National Intelligence Estimate that he "did not see how analysts could have come up with a different conclusion about Iraq's WMD based on the intelligence available at the time."

Henry S. Rowen, a former Pentagon official in the first Bush administration, sat on the Robb-Silberman commission. "I remember his [Pillar's] *Foreign Affairs* article and I read it with great interest," Rowen told me. "I thought, 'How about an example or an incident or something specific?' I don't remember it being there."

Rowen said the commission set up a hotline and advertised it throughout the intelligence community. Anyone could phone in a tip anonymously. No one called. "We looked as thoroughly as we could into the question of political pressure and we basically drew a blank, so if he had something to say he sure didn't say anything to us that was persuasive."

(I should point out here that the 2002 NIE that Bush's critics persist in saying was the product of political pressure was not that different from intelligence assessments under President Clinton. A 1999 joint intelligence report stated, "We believe that Iraq possesses chemical agent stockpiles that can be, or already are, weaponized." Two months before Bush took office, the intelligence community said, "Our main judgments about what remains of Iraq's original WMD programs, agent stockpiles, and delivery systems have changed little. Iraq retains stockpiles of chemical and biological agents and munitions.")

The fact that Pillar bucked two bipartisan panels—and himself—did not stop liberal journalists from promoting the latest charges from an ex-CIA analyst. No story I saw on his *Foreign Affairs* article mentioned the two panels' findings or Pillar's testimony about the 2002 NIE as a contrast to what he was writing in 2006.

Pillar then moved to Georgetown University to teach national security issues. During an interview, he bristled when I asked if Congressman Pete Hoekstra and other conservatives were correct in calling the CIA a leak machine targeting Bush. "You touched a hot button," he said. "You see a leap of logic that isn't very logical."

"There might be a hallway worth of leakers out at Langley and Fort Meade. I don't know. . . . [But] people who work at an agency like the CIA and NSA have to take things like periodic reinvestigations. Polygraphs. They are going to be far more antsy about leaking information than other people."

As the CIA's top Middle East analyst, Pillar worked on the 2002 NIE, but not the part that dealt with Iraq's weapons of mass destruction. He conceded he had no proof of political pressure, referring instead to a "political environment" that contributed to "analytical errors." Told of the Robb-Silberman passage that quotes him as saying evidence justified the NIE, he said, "I think the point to take away, given the reporting such as it was, the most plausible interpretation was not that there were no weapons programs at all."

He said that his 2003 talk at SAIS had been mostly positive except for his criticism of Bush's linkage of terrorism and WMD. He justified his criticism of Bush in his 2004 talk in California as reflecting the collapsing situation in Iraq, but declined to discuss other talks he made during his CIA tenure or identify the audience.

As I interviewed Pillar, it became clear he was unaware that the Senate Intelligence Committee report had said that the CIA had not warned White House National Security Council officials about the "sixteen words" in Bush's 2003 State of the Union speech. When I told him about the committee finding, he replied, "Sounds like, 'He said, she said.'"

Finally, Pillar asserted to me that Langley is a bipartisan place. "You can see Democratic bumper stickers out at the parking lot at Langley as well as Republican ones."

TYLER DRUMHELLER

CBS's award-winning *60 Minutes* has served for years as a perch for Republican critics. Days before the 2004 election, the show planned to broadside Bush with a story on a neglected weapons depot south of Baghdad, giving him little time to respond. But Internet bloggers outed the story before it aired, and Bush and his conservative media allies had time to rebut the charges.

It was no surprise, then, that *60 Minutes* became a forum for disgruntled ex-CIA officers, Tyler Drumheller among them. In the spring of 2006, Drumheller became the latest Langley alumnus to hurl charges at the Bush administration. Republican senators took note and later accused Drumheller of falsehoods. Drumheller was continuing a pattern that had begun in 2002. The intelligence community, sometimes anonymously, sometimes not, would make allegations of Bush administration wrongdoing. The charges were leaked to the press. Months later, the Senate Intelligence Committee or another body would find no evidence to back up the leaks. But by then, the damage to the public's perception of the war had been done.

Drumheller's allegation centered on Iraqi foreign minister Naji Sabri. Sabri had direct access to Saddam Hussein. To the delight of the CIA, Sabri became its spy before the March 2003 invasion. The CIA's clandestine service considered the source so sensitive that it did not share Sabri's information with the analytical service, and thus we can presume it was not used to bolster the flawed 2002 NIE on Iraq.

Until his retirement in 2005 Drumheller ran the CIA's European stations from Langley. He knew firsthand about Sabri. CIA director George Tenet, he said, delivered the news—that Sabri said Saddam had no WMD—personally to the White House. Then Drumheller made the following statements to *60 Minutes* correspondent Ed Bradley, as millions watched.

Drumheller: He told us that they had no active weapons of mass destruction program.

Bradley: So in the fall of 2002, before going to war, we had it on good authority from a source within Saddam's inner circle that he didn't have an active program for weapons of mass destruction?

Drumheller: Yes.

Bradley: It directly contradicts, though, what the president and his staff were telling us.

> **Drumheller:** The policy was set. The war in Iraq was coming. And
> they were looking for intelligence to fit into the policy, to justify the
> policy.

It was an astonishing charge: Bush had gone to war even though weeks
before the invasion a member of Saddam's inner circle had said there were
no WMD.

It was a great scoop for the anti-Bush CBS, the same news organization
that had vouched for fake Texas Air National Guard documents in an attempt
to besmirch Bush before the 2004 election. Drumheller went on other television shows to make his charge, all in a prelude to his book.

Trouble is, Drumheller's story is not true. In fact, the opposite is true. Senator Pat Roberts directed the Intelligence Committee staff to collect every bit
of reporting the CIA owned on Sabri's information. The staff found that
Sabri, rather than debunking the idea that Iraq had WMD, actually affirmed
that it did.

"All of the information about this case so far indicates that the information from this source was that Iraq did have WMD programs," Roberts wrote
in the fall of 2006. Tenet, by then no longer CIA director, privately told the
committee that Drumheller "mischaracterized" Sabri's information. Roberts
obtained copies of the CIA's reporting on Sabri at the time. The documents
stated the exact opposite of what Drumheller had said on *60 Minutes*. Iraq
was "aggressively and covertly" developing a nuclear weapon, Sabri said, and
was currently producing chemical weapons.

Drumheller's CIA associates considered him a compulsive liar. When I
asked a Senate Republican about him, the aide replied, "Drumheller is full of
shit." The blunt assessments stem from this fact: the *60 Minutes* appearance
was not the first time Drumheller had spun a tale.

On this point, the Drumheller story begins with an Iraqi defector known by the codename "Curveball." A chemical engineer, Curveball defected to Germany in 1998 and promised inside information on Saddam's system of mobile bioweapons laboratories. His information got better and better as the Germans dangled permanent residence status as a reward. The Germans wrote scores of reports on their findings and shared them with the U.S.

Curveball, like some other Iraqi sources, turned out to be a fraud. His story, via German intelligence, became the prime basis for the CIA's assertion in the 2002 NIE that Iraq still dabbled in germ warfare. The story of Curveball has been told by both the Senate Intelligence Committee and the Robb-Silberman commission. What has not been told is Drumheller's full behind-the-scenes role.

A senior CIA officer told me Drumheller played both sides of the field. When Curveball was deemed a crucial source, Drumheller promoted him. When Curveball was discredited, Drumheller switched sides, claiming he had warned the Agency about him. The following was revealed to me by a CIA officer.

In December 1999 the CIA station in Berlin sent a cable to its German counterpart asking for access to Curveball. The Germans replied with five major points: no access; his information is plausible; Germany cannot verify; please protect the source; you can use the information. Drumheller read the memo and then reported orally up the chain of command: you can use the information and protect the source. He left out the other three stipulations. A month later, the CIA German station chief wrote a cable to Drumheller questioning Curveball's reliability. The cable never reached Tenet.

In 2002, Drumheller met with the German intelligence station chief in Washington. Over lunch, the German told him that Curveball was a single source, and that there was no one to back up his information.

Drumheller told the Robb-Silberman commission a far different story, which also appeared in his book. He quoted the station chief as telling him: "Well, just between us, and I'll deny it if it ever comes out, we have a lot of doubts about this guy. He's a very erratic character. We've had to move him a couple of times. And it's a single source whose reporting can't be validated and I personally think he could be a fabricator."

The senior intelligence officer I interviewed about Drumheller told me the German denied to the CIA that he had ever made such statements. He said he never used the word "fabricator" nor said most of the things attributed to him by Drumheller. There is no record of any memo in which Drumheller recounted this interview for anyone at the CIA.

In his memoir, Tenet takes on Drumheller directly, recounting times when Drumheller uttered allegations that did not match the facts. Tenet wrote that if the German counterpart had actually said these derogatory things about Curveball, and Drumheller had reported them, it would have dramatically changed the Iraq NIE then in process.

But there was no Drumheller report. Tenet said neither Drumheller or any other official told him of such a conversation. "No such report was disseminated, nor was the issue ever brought to my attention," Tenet wrote. "In fact, I've been told that subsequent investigations have produced not a single piece of paper anywhere at CIA documenting Drumheller's meeting with the German." He said the first he ever heard of Drumheller's German story was when he was questioned by the Robb-Silberman commission.

There are other examples of Drumheller telling what CIA officers believed were falsehoods in order to make himself appear as the man who tried to blow the whistle on Curveball.

Drumheller claimed before the Robb-Silberman commission that when he saw a draft copy of Colin Powell's February 2003 presentation to the UN on Iraqi WMD, he deleted Curveball's information. No CIA employee recalls ever seeing such a redacted version.

Drumheller told the commission he called the deputy CIA director's office to make an appointment to discuss Curveball. The deputy director's assistant said no such call ever took place.

Drumheller told the commission he subsequently did meet with deputy CIA director John McLaughlin and warned him that Curveball was a fabricator. McLaughlin said no meeting took place. There was no entry about meeting with Drumheller in his official calendar.

Drumheller also drew George Tenet into his claims. He told the commission that on the night before Colin Powell's speech, Tenet telephoned him to obtain the phone number of another foreign intelligence service. Drumheller said that during this midnight call he warned the director about Curveball's unreliability. Tenet told the commission there had, in fact, been no discussion of Curveball.

In short, no one remembers the meetings or conservations Drumheller says he had on Curveball.

In his book Drumheller concludes, "It seems to me now that I could hardly have made it clearer that Curveball was not to be trusted, but it did not matter. My doubts stood no chance of being heard."

Drumheller makes no mention of the Sabri affair. The book contains this publisher's note: "Material about a *60 Minutes* investigation of the pre-invasion period in Iraq has been deleted to satisfy CIA vetting requirements." The publisher released the book before Senator Roberts essentially labeled Drumheller a liar in his committee's September 2006 report.

Drumheller declined my repeated requests for an interview. He is listed in Federal Election Commission records as a campaign contributor to two Democratic senators.

Curveball was another bad source relied on by the intelligence community. It should be pointed out that it was during Clinton's administration, not Bush's, that Curveball's reporting began. His information in 1999 and 2000 made its way into several intelligence products asserting that Iraq maintained a germ warfare program.

Even after Roberts had published CIA intelligence reports that showed Drumheller had said the complete opposite of what Sabri had told him, the media still sought him out for comment.

After Kyle "Dusty" Foggo, a close aide to then CIA director Porter Goss, was indicted on bribery charges in February 2007, ABC asked Drumheller for an assessment. "In an organization of professional liars, we have to be honest with each other. So if the charges are true, it's a betrayal of everything the Agency stands for," he said. "It's a sad day for Dusty and a sad day for the Agency."

Thus did Tyler Drumheller—considered by his associates to be "full of shit," with a record of grossly misleading the media and the public about Curveball and about other bad Iraqi sources—become, in the media's eyes, the conscience of the intelligence community.

ALUMNI HALL

By the winter of 2003, the CIA's PR war on Bush had broadened. A group of current and former intelligence officers formed an anti-Bush organization called Veteran Intelligence Professionals for Sanity. Leading the group were Ray McGovern and Bill Christison, both of whom gave support to the unfounded conspiracy theory that the U.S. government executed the September 11 attacks. Another member was Patrick Lang, an ex-DIA officer known for his consistent attacks on Bush. The organization says most of its CIA members come from the analytical side—analysts from Langley headquarters rather than agents in the field. McGovern told me that its members include not just retirees but "more than a handful" of current CIA employ-

ees. His group has fifty-nine members, all told; McGovern declined to identify those still active in the CIA.

The group's first major act was to sign a February 2003 letter to President
Bush opposing the impending Iraq war. Interestingly, one of their arguments
was that Saddam would use his chemical weapons stocks. Like everyone else,
these hardened intelligence professionals believed Iraq still harbored weapons
of mass destruction.

As time went on, some of these ex-CIA officers began crossing the line
from criticizing Bush's foreign policy to endorsing the views of far-out conspiracy theorists. Both Christison and McGovern have endorsed the idea that
the September 11, 2001, attacks were part of a conspiracy.

McGovern moderated a talk at the University of California–Berkeley by
some of the leading conspiracy proponents. At a peace rally in Washington,
McGovern zeroed in on American Flight 77, the plane that hit the Pentagon.
"Is there a cover-up? Yes," he told a cheering crowd of antiwar demonstrators.
"The question is: what's being covered up?"

Then he took his allegations up a notch. "Why do you think the vice president let that plane, or whatever it was, hit the Pentagon?"

In one sentence, a former CIA employee, one so senior he used to brief the
White House personally, endorsed the crazy idea that the vice president of
the United States might have had a hand in allowing or even planning the
September 11 attacks. He likewise gave credence to those who contend that
a missile, not a plane, hit the west façade.

McGovern told the anti-Bush gathering that Cheney was informed of the
plane's path for forty minutes as it approached Washington, but never took
action. This, in fact, is not what happened. The 9-11 Commission reported
that the White House, where Cheney hunkered down in a command center,
was not informed of the airliner's approach until 9:34 a.m., three minutes
before it struck. Secret Service agents then moved the vice president to a
below-ground room at about the same time the Pentagon was struck. When

Cheney received tracking information on the last surviving hijacked plane, United Flight 93, he gave the order to shoot it down, but the commission determined that the order never reached airborne fighter pilots before passengers heroically brought the plane down in Pennsylvania.

Months later, I asked McGovern if he really thought Vice President Cheney "let" a plane hit the Pentagon.

"I may have misspoken," he said. "I don't see enough evidence to accuse or indict Cheney on 9/11." Then I asked the man who has hosted conferences on such conspiracies if he really believes something other than a plane crashed into the Pentagon. "There is so much conflicting testimony on that," he said. "I think it's probable that a plane hit the Pentagon. . . . Right now the evidence is not strong enough to validate any of these [alternative] theories."

AT THE WHITE HOUSE

The CIA alumni struck again at Bush in 2006, this time in the person of Flynt Leverett. Leverett worked as a Middle East analyst at Langley. Headquarters detailed him to the White House National Security Council staff to work on war policy. The White House did not choose Leverett, which was not unusual. More than 80 percent of the NSC staff consists of people sent from other agencies or departments. Rather than the White House selecting the staff, agencies are expected to cough up "volunteers," and Leverett was the CIA's. He was interviewed and accepted.

It was not a good fit. The NSC was a bastion of neoconservative policymakers. There were few priorities higher than protecting Israel. They espoused a doctrine of not talking directly to terrorist states like Syria and Iran. Leverett viewed Iran as mostly benign; he thought the United States should open talks with the militant Muslim theocracy that was sending powerful explosives into Iraq to kill American troops. He also advocated putting more pressure on Israel to negotiate with and make concessions to the Palestinians.

Leverett worked under Zalmay Khalilzad, who would go on to be ambassador to Afghanistan and Iraq. But at interagency meetings, Leverett stunned participants by declaring himself in charge of Middle East policy. "I decide what the policy is," he declared at a meeting on Iran and Syria. He openly dismissed others' opinions. His colleagues spoke of his arrogance.

On June 24, 2002, Bush walked out to the Rose Garden to announce a major new policy. He became the first president to endorse a Palestinian state. Flanked by Condoleezza Rice, Colin Powell, and Donald Rumsfeld, Bush declared, "In the [current] situation the Palestinian people will grow more and more miserable. My vision is two states, living side by side in peace and security. . . . Peace requires a new and different Palestinian leadership, so that a Palestinian state can be born."

Bush was calling for a democratic Palestinian state, with someone other than Yasser Arafat at the helm. While Bush's step was dramatic, Leverett declared it was not enough and actively opposed administration policy. He was eased out of the White House in 2003. He soon started speaking and writing against the administration, especially regarding the administration's policy on Iran.

In the Bush administration's view, Iran's radical mullahs have stood at the center of terrorism since seizing power in 1979. The Iranians are working to develop weapons; they want to annihilate Israel; they want to impose a radical Shi'ite regime in Lebanon; and they fund Hezbollah, which has killed more Americans than any other terror group except al Qaeda. But to Leverett's way of thinking, Iran and its bellicose president Mahmoud Ahmadinejad are misunderstood victims of the Bush and Cheney hard-liners. Here are a few samples of his writings from the *New York Times*:

> Iran will not help the United States in Iraq because it wants to avoid chaos there.

Tehran cooperated with United States efforts in Afghanistan primarily because it wanted a better relationship with Washington.

If President Bush does not move decisively toward strategic engagement with Tehran during his remaining two years in office, his successor will not have the same opportunities that he will have so blithely squandered.

If this was the advice Leverett was tendering to the administration while he was at the NSC, and if it represents the thinking of the CIA, it's not so hard to see Langley not as the administration's chief intelligence agency but as a foreign policy opponent of the administration.

These men—Pillar, Drumheller, and Leverett—were typical in one respect: they were all career CIA.

CHAPTER 5

REVOLT AT LANGLEY

"[CIA director George Tenet] was either unwilling or unable to marshal the full range of intelligence community resources necessary to combat the growing threat to the United States.... The record of this joint inquiry indicates that [Tenet] *did not* marshal resources effectively even within the CIA against the threat posed by al Qaeda.

Despite the DCI's declaration to the CIA officials that the agency was at war with bin Laden, there is substantial evidence that the DCI's Counterterrorist Center needed additional personnel prior to September 11, and that the lack of resources had a substantial impact on its ability to detect and monitor al Qaeda activities."

Joint Inquiry into Intelligence Community Activities Before and After the Terrorist Attacks of September 11, 2001, December 2002 final report

Porter Goss headed to Langley to run the CIA with a carrot and a stick. Gone was George Tenet, who had ruled Langley longer than any director except the fabled Allen Dulles. President Bush had relied on Clinton's four-year CIA director for some of the most important wartime intelligence assessments in the nation's history.

Tenet had lobbied to stay on in 2000. He had worked to officially name the CIA compound the George Bush Center for Intelligence, after the president's father, who briefly ran the CIA in the 1970s. Tenet formed a close working relationship with the second Bush. He acceded to the president's wish that he brief him personally each day, eschewing the historical practice of sending a professional analyst. Tenet would show up at the White House with a thick black binder containing the President's Daily Brief. But intelligence scandals and investigations dominated his Bush years, and by 2004, a weary Tenet wanted out. And some in the administration wanted him to go. They believed that in keeping Tenet, Bush had left himself without an advocate at Langley.

Analysts and case officers had absorbed three years of rhetorical punishment since the September 11 attacks. Critics blamed the CIA for failing to penetrate the September 11 plot, misjudging Iraq's WMD, leaking to the press, and condoning incompetence within the ranks.

Congressman Porter Goss, who had been a stern critic of the CIA's performance, seemed a CIA director in waiting. A former Army intelligence officer, Goss had been recruited by the CIA and worked on clandestine operations in Latin America. He retired in 1971 after almost dying of blood poisoning. He then went into business in Florida, entered politics, and was elected to the U.S. House in 1988. Ten years later, his colleagues made him House Intelligence Committee chairman. A sturdy Republican with deep intelligence experience, Goss seemed just the man to look out for Bush's interests.

With Goss confirmed by the Senate, the Langley bureaucracy braced for more turmoil. Months before he arrived at the CIA, he had approved a blistering attack (in the House committee's unclassified budget report) on the performance of the Agency's clandestine service.

"All is not well in the world of clandestine human intelligence collection (HUMINT)," the blunt report read. "For too long the CIA has been ignoring its core mission activities. There is a dysfunctional denial of any need for corrective action." It was a shot at Tenet's leadership and a direct hit on Stephen Kappes, who as director of operations ran the CIA's network of case officers and spies abroad. Goss's staff put even more biting criticism in the report's secret addendum. It was based on the reporting of investigators who had visited CIA stations and talked to scores of officers. The public report said the clandestine service had been decimated under Bill Clinton and stood five years away, at best, from being put back together. The CIA was misusing its experienced field officers, not listening to their recommendations, and bristling at any outside criticism.

A senior intelligence official told me that the CIA clandestine service, more than a decade after the Cold War's end, had still not adjusted to the new reality. It had relied on embassies, where clandestine officers worked under diplomatic cover, as virtually the only bases of operation. It had not developed more creative ways for case officers to recruit spies. This lack of creative thinking really hit home after the September 11 attacks. The Bush administration needed information from Afghanistan, Iraq, Iran, and North Korea. America had no embassies in any of these states, and, not coincidentally, next to no intelligence on them from the CIA. The CIA had failed to penetrate al Qaeda, knew little about the inside workings of the Taliban, and had (and has) few contacts inside Iran. The CIA relied instead on electronic means of gathering intelligence and on defectors.

Few in the Agency spoke Arabic. During the Cold War it was less important if a case officer didn't speak Russian. Soviet bloc military commanders used common phrases for orders, and a language-deficient case officer could pick up a few Slavic phrases (if not a crash course in Russian) and be okay. But al Qaeda operatives speak in code words in different dialects. For example, "I'm taking oranges to the dinner" could actually mean "I have plans for the attack." During the Cold War, establishing cover outside an embassy was not that important in areas like Central and South America. An officer could throw cash around and get plenty of information. In most Muslim countries, especially in al Qaeda–infested areas, establishing cover and getting information was much more difficult. An American throwing cash around in Jalalabad would not go unnoticed.

During his Senate confirmation hearings, Goss said he planned to shake up the clandestine service with "blunt, strong language," about its performance. "I don't like doing it. . . . But I think occasionally you have to do that."

What the public did not know in 2004 was the sorry state of the CIA's Baghdad station. With more than five hundred analysts, case officers, and ex-agents working on contract, the CIA's station in Baghdad (which was in the American embassy) came to be Langley's largest. The demand for intelligence inside Iraq was so great that Langley closed other stations around the world in order to shift resources to Baghdad. (One officer commented, "The CIA no longer has global reach.")

In early 2004, before Goss took control, deputy director of operations James Pavitt visited the Baghdad station. Alarmed at the lack of morale and production, he replaced the station chief. Public reports blamed the firing on leaks—station cables had shown up in the *New York Times* days after they were written. But in a closed hearing, Pavitt told the Senate Intelligence Committee that the leaks had nothing to do with his decision.

There were other problems. I learned of major disputes between CIA station chiefs in Pakistan and Afghanistan. One such dispute let one of the most wanted Taliban members get away.

Running military and CIA operations along the border in both countries is a complex mix of diplomacy, turf battles, intrigue, and deception. Pakistani president Pervez Musharraf lets the CIA operate hundreds of paramilitary forces and officers in his country, but not uniformed U.S. personnel. The Islamabad CIA station has a big say on when the military in Afghanistan can cross into Pakistan to pursue Taliban or al Qaeda operatives.

One night in the fall of 2005, this mishmash of rules came back to bite the United States. One of the chief targets of the Joint Special Operations Command (JSOC), the nation's premier terrorist-hunting agency, is Ahmad Shah, a Taliban leader who calls himself Commander Ismail. He leads hundreds of fighters who move in and out of Afghanistan's Kunar Province, east of Kabul on the Pakistan border.

The military believe Shah's men ambushed and killed three Navy SEALs, members of JSOC who were on a reconnaissance mission in Kunar. Shah later told NBC that his band not only killed the SEALs, but also then laid an ambush for the Chinook helicopter that came to their aid. He said he knew the Americans would send help. When it approached, they shot it down with a rocket-propelled grenade, killing all sixteen Americans aboard.

That December night, the National Security Agency picked up Shah's voice on a satellite phone. The U.S. had his phone number. He was a few miles inside Pakistan, and he talked to a friend about coming back into Kunar. The NSA uses a ground-based classified eavesdropping system, satellites, and Predator unmanned air vehicles to suck up communications. Based on the signals and GPS coordinates, the CIA's station in Kabul believed JSOC could dispatch a team a few miles over the border to get Shah. But the CIA station in Pakistan balked, saying it should run the mission even though its men were more than sixty miles away. There were shouting matches over the phone. No mission was launched. Shah escaped.

GEORGE TENET

Goss's arrival at Langley that September felt like an invasion. Gone was George Tenet, the affable cigar-chomping son of Greek immigrants, a schmoozer and back-slapper who often burst into a room with an amusing quip. In was Porter Goss, the bespectacled Ivy Leaguer who had promised to give the agency a tongue-lashing, who had criticized it, and who had brought a group of trusted congressional aides determined to change the way things were done.

Tenet had sat in the director's seventh-floor office for seven years and had become an agency icon. Visitors could see him in a long leather trench coat chewing cigars outside the building, cajoling the staff. His favorite overseas destination was London, where MI6 directors treated him like a visiting head of state and entertained him in the city's cushiony men's clubs. There, Tenet could chomp cigars and share gossip. Later, MI6 would share some of these tidbits with other European intelligence services in a way that sent a message: we are the ones with the special relationship with America, not you.

Tenet knew the CIA's power was in its operations branch. He went out of his way to praise clandestine officers and stayed in touch with retired chiefs and directors. He knew that keeping his people happy was the way to keep negative stories out of the *Washington Post* and the *New York Times*.

Tenet's affable style got mixed results. It worked with President Bush, who enjoyed being personally briefed by Tenet every morning. But officers at the CIA felt that Tenet, in the process, had lost his professional detachment and become part of the White House club. And some senators—like Republican Richard Shelby, a domineering Alabama politician who preceded Pat Roberts as Intelligence Committee chairman—looked passed the schmoozing and saw a poor manager.

One of the lasting images of director Tenet was his head bobbing in agreement as he sat behind Secretary of State Colin Powell. The scene was the United Nations Security Council, February 2003, a month before the invasion of Iraq. Bush had picked Powell, a man of enormous diplomatic stature, to travel to Langley to hear Tenet's evidence that Saddam Hussein still owned weapons of mass destruction. Powell put his credibility on the line as the world watched him make the case for war at the UN.

Powell's words, the ones Tenet endorsed with a bobbing head, turned out to be mostly wrong. Worst, some of the evidence presented to Powell during his trip to Langley came from sources who had been labeled fabricators by the Agency itself. Yet their "evidence" had not been deleted from the presentation. The CIA did not tell Powell some of the evidence came from liars.

After Powell resigned as secretary of state, he said his UN performance was something he would have to live with the rest of his life. Of Tenet, he told a colleague, "If I could slit his throat, I would."

GOSS AT THE HELM

By the fall of 2004, Goss was in charge at Langley. His inner circle consisted of the same congressional aides who wrote the scathing denunciation of CIA spying. Among them was Michael Kostiw, who had been staff director of the terrorism subcommittee of the House Permanent Select Committee on Intelligence under Goss. Kostiw had also been a longtime CIA case officer during the Cold War. He was the only veteran of the clandestine service among Goss's closest aides. Goss dispatched Kostiw to Iraq to find out the truth about the war. Pat Murray, a former federal prosecutor who had been Goss's Intelligence Committee staff director, became Goss's chief of staff. And Jay Jakub, another top congressional staffer, became his senior advisor on operations and analysis.

These invaders would now carry out Goss's orders to shake up the place. They soon found that the Agency was leaking like a sieve against them. The stories all had the same plotline: Goss's people were incompetent, partisan, and evil; the Langley workforce was being victimized.

As one of his first acts as director, Goss gave a speech to staff in the "bubble," the CIA's super-secure auditorium. He centered on three topics. First, he wanted thorough and timely collection and analysis of intelligence. Second, he didn't want the Agency to focus narrowly on counter-terrorism; he wanted a "global approach" that looked at every global threat. And finally, he wanted the leaks to stop. To that end, Goss ordered the Agency's inspector general, John Helgerson, to cast a wide net for leakers; investigations would involve interrogation and polygraphs. This last item was the stick Goss had brought to the CIA.

But rather than beating the Agency into compliance, Goss and his staff found that the atmosphere grew ever more hostile. They even found themselves whispering one day in the director's office, as if they were surrounded by the enemy. They laughed about it when they recognized what they were doing, but it was telling that they felt compelled to do it in the first place.

When Goss arrived, Helgerson was finishing up an accountability review of the September 11 attacks. The report was never made public, but apparently it placed individual blame on many in the Agency, leading right up to Tenet himself, and justified disciplinary punishments. When the inspector general completed his report in 2005, Goss contemplated setting up disciplinary boards, but he was incapable of firing anyone. Instead, Goss pardoned the entire workforce. This was the carrot. After the announcement, he arrived on the seventh floor, heading to his office. Along the corridor, relieved workers gave him a standing ovation. But some officers grumbled that if the CIA was not held accountable for mistakes, it would never reform. In the end, no one was punished for the intelligence failures leading to the September 11, 2001, attacks.

BUNGLED OPERATIONS

The public did not have to take Goss's word on the sorry state of the clandestine service. They only needed to pick up a newspaper. Perhaps the most glaring case of ineptitude happened in northern Italy in the winter of 2003. The city of Milan is known for fashion and food, but it was full of intrigue that winter. A contingent of twelve CIA officers was searching for a suspected al Qaeda chieftain, an Egyptian named Hassan Mustafa Osama Nasr, or Abu Omar. The mission: apprehend him and transfer him to another country, such as Jordan or Egypt, where he could be held and interrogated. This process is known as "extraordinary rendition." Used little before September 11, the snatch operation had become fairly routine, a quick, clean way to take al Qaeda terrorists out of commission absent the niceties of a court hearing and formal charges.

The operation in Milan, however, was anything but quick and clean. Operating with the cooperation of Italian intelligence, the American officers were supposed to use codenames. But some of them used their own credit cards to pay hotel bills, wanting the frequent flyer miles. They also used their personal cell phones to call home, leaving an undeniable record of their locations. Still, they managed to grab Omar off the streets and fly him to the U.S. air base at Ramstein, Germany, and then to Egypt.

Jeff Castelli, the Rome bureau chief at the time, briefed Langley on what a success the mission had been. But the thrill was short-lived. After the Egyptians found they did not have enough evidence to hold Omar, they released him. He went public, accusing the CIA of criminal abduction. Italian prosecutors then sprang into action. Capitalizing on the CIA's sloppy tradecraft, they learned the officers' names and filed charges. The dozen or so officers involved, including Castelli, fled to Langley. Some retired. Some took on new jobs. Milan stands as one of the most bungled CIA operations in recent memory, and as an embarrassment to President Bush.

A CIA officer told me that what is significant about the Milan debacle is not the poor spycraft but the fact the CIA even launched the operation in the first place. It had obviously failed to put together the proper evidence to hold Omar, and the CIA must have been dreaming if it thought that the Italian government would let it execute a kidnapping without ramifications. The Italian judicial system is vigorously independent. America would not tolerate a foreign intelligence service snatching someone off U.S. streets; why did the Rome station chief think Italy would look the other way?

If the Milan operation exposed flawed CIA thinking, a reprise in Macedonia revealed pure hubris. The agency wanted to snatch another suspected

Islamic militant, Khaled el-Masri. A German citizen, el-Masri was in Macedonia when local authorities grabbed him at the CIA's request. The CIA flew him to a prison in Afghanistan, where he was interrogated for weeks. Eventually, the debriefers learned they had the wrong man. This el-Masri might have had some questionable contacts, but he was not the el-Masri tied to al Qaeda. What is worse, according to a CIA clandestine officer who agreed to talk to me on condition of anonymity and no direct quotes, is that the Agency officers who oversaw the snatch knew the man was probably not the real McCoy. But, the officer said, they went after him anyway just to show that they could do a daring rendition, and because it's fun to run operations and report to Langley that you did great things. The CIA flew el-Masri to Albania, gave him some cash, and let him go. He has since filed a lawsuit against the Agency. German authorities are investigating. Again the CIA had flaunted a European country's rule of law, and it paid the price in the exposure of another botched mission.

THE CLINTON DISASTER

Much of the blame for the decrepit state of the CIA's operations and its faulty analysis can be traced to the Clinton administration and its eight years of eroding the Agency. Searching for a post–Cold War peace dividend, Clinton did more than slash the military. He targeted the intelligence community. He shrank the CIA's analytical and operations branches by at least 30 percent. Stations in Latin America and Asia closed or downsized. Indonesia, the world's largest Muslim country, had only three CIA officers by the mid-1990s. The entire roster of case officers was reduced from 1,600 to 1,200, and there were only 400 collection management officers at American embassies to turn reports from case officers into cables back to Langley.

In this atmosphere, station officers knew that if you wanted to get promoted you had to move from country to country. It looked good on a résumé. But such careerism left the Agency woefully short of officers with deep expertise on certain countries or regions. The number of cables flowing to Langley dropped dramatically. As a result, the CIA knew far less about the world than it ever had.

Guatemala is a good example of the effects of the Clinton culture. Not only did Clinton cut the spy ranks, but he also did not want the Agency dealing with unsavory characters. It was a tall order, as the shadowy task of recruiting agents often found CIA officers plumbing the depths to get information. In Central America, the CIA paid a Guatemalan colonel for regular information on Communists and drug runners. But when the colonel was linked to the deaths of two Americans, his status as a paid agent was revealed in 1995 by then congressman Bob Torricelli, a New Jersey Democrat. The CIA stopped paying him. And to make sure it was not caught up in another Central American scandal, a CIA clandestine officer told me, the Agency cut off ties to virtually all its Guatemalan agents in Central America. It also closed its bases and some stations, leaving the United States with very little intelligence on Central America.

The outing of the Guatemalan agent spawned the "Torricelli Principle." Director John Deutch decreed that case officers could no longer recruit agents. The source had to be approved by senior people at Langley. If the potential agent was not absolutely pure and clean, he had little chance of getting on the payroll.

James Woolsey, Clinton's first CIA director (who resigned in protest over President Clinton's apparent lack of interest in the CIA), later told Congress the new rule stank.

"These rules make absolutely no sense with respect to terrorist groups because the only people who are in terrorist groups are people who want to be terrorists," Woolsey testified. "That means they have a background in violence and human rights violations."

"If you make it difficult for a CIA case officer in, say, Beirut, to recruit spies with this sort of background, he'll be able to do a dandy job for you, telling you what's going on inside, for example, the churches and the chambers of commerce of Beirut, but we don't really care what's going on there. He'll have no idea, however, what's going on inside Hezbollah."

Republicans expressed outrage at Torricelli's unilateral outing of the Guatemalan general. But Clinton dismissed the affair. Asked by reporters if he was concerned about exposing an agent, the president said, "I am concerned about the information coming out, but, in the end, I think that it is unlikely given the facts of this case that certain information would not have come out." Pro-defense conservatives asked how the CIA could recruit sources if the sources knew that lawmakers in Washington could release their names at any time and put them in danger.

By the mid-1990s, the CIA had virtually stopped recruiting new case officers. It began paying veteran spies to quit. The clandestine service had few middle-level experienced case officers to spread around. Officers either were very old or very young. In 1995, Clinton issued a new directive, called Presidential Decision Directive 35. Agency veterans were astounded. The directive listed three priorities for the sixteen agencies that make up the intelligence community. First was supporting the military. Second was to focus on countries that posed an obvious threat to American security interests. The third was a catchall. Under the heading of "transnational threats," the CIA was to look at drug trafficking, weapons proliferation, organized crime, and terrorism. At the very time U.S. spies needed to be everywhere, the CIA was pulling back.

When Defense Secretary William Cohen issued his final defense strategy to Congress—just months before the September 11 attacks—he listed terrorism among a grab bag of threats, including sea piracy. The Clinton Pentagon did not single out bin Laden, who had declared war on America in 1998, or al Qaeda, as specific threats, even though al Qaeda had already repeatedly attacked American targets abroad.

Overall, the Clinton administration appeared to regard the CIA as a Cold War relic. And its "peace dividend" downsizing of the CIA left America vulnerable. The CIA closed scores of bases in the 1990s, including the one in Hamburg, Germany, where Mohamed Atta and his friends planned the September 11 attacks. (After the attack, the CIA reappeared in Hamburg—a hotbed of radical Muslim ideology—but only with a one-officer base.) So it is no surprise that the CIA failed to penetrate the September 11 plot. As Osama bin Laden was building al Qaeda into an international Islamic terror organization determined to kill Americans, Clinton was crippling the CIA.

The Clinton administration's shrinking of the CIA must be factored into the erroneous 2002 National Intelligence Estimate on Iraq's weapons. The CIA had no agents inside the Iraqi regime. As one CIA clandestine officer told me, if the CIA had really wanted sources close to Saddam, it should have cultivated them twenty or thirty years ago. It had not. The CIA had been in retreat ever since 1975, when Senator Frank Church's committee on intelligence not only exposed CIA misdeeds, but also severely hobbled its ability to recruit agents. This process was only made worse by the Clinton administration's policies. So in Saddam Hussein's Iraq, the CIA found itself relying on dubious defectors who, as in the case of downed pilot Scott Speicher, lied for cash.

Another hit to CIA morale was the Clinton administration's lax approach to security. Violators were not punished if they were Clinton appointees. Clinton pardoned a historian who stole classified photos and gave them to *Jane's*, an intelligence consulting group, for dissemination. Woolsey's successor at the CIA, John Deutch, ran afoul of CIA rules when it was discovered that he kept classified documents on unsecured laptop computers that he took home. Deutch faced possible prosecution, but Clinton pardoned him at the end of his second term. A decade later, Clinton defended his former national security advisor, Sandy Berger. During the 9-11 Commission investigation, Berger went to the National Archives to steal secret Clinton-era documents demanded by the panel. He was seen stuffing documents into his socks and hiding them outside the building. He later admitted to destroying them at his law office. Clinton, however, excused Berger by saying it was all part of his former aide's rumpled, disorganized style. What it was really in keeping with was the Clinton administration's irresponsible approach to national security.

In a speech in Dallas in the spring of 2007, Defense Secretary Robert Gates, a former CIA director, provided a glimpse into the Clinton years.

"By the mid-1990s, recruitment of new case officers at CIA had hit a historic low, and the agency's funding was a prime target for budget-cutters," he said. "Indeed, within three years of my retirement in 1993, CIA's clandestine service had been cut by 30 percent—just when Osama bin Laden was gearing up his war on the United States."

But a more devastating criticism came that spring, this one from Clinton's own CIA director. In his memoir, George Tenet wrote, "The fact is that by the mid-to-late 1990s American intelligence was in Chapter 11, and neither Congress nor the executive branch did much about it."

Tenet disclosed that he personally asked Clinton for billions more in budget dollars as the al Qaeda threat grew. No increase came. "You can't toss spies at al Qaeda when you don't have them, especially when you lack the recruiting and training infrastructure to get them and grow them," the former director wrote. His assessment of the NSA, on which the nation relied to hear critical conversations that could have tipped off the September 11 plot, was even more dire: "You don't simply tell NSA to give you more signals intelligence when their capabilities are crumbling and they are 'going deaf,' unable to monitor critical voice communications," he said of the NSA in the late 1990s.

Here it was, straight from Clinton's own man. Bill Clinton had let the CIA and NSA degrade to dangerous levels.

IRAQ DEBACLE

All this history came crashing down on the CIA's Baghdad station during the Iraq war. Officers returning to Langley recounted the problem: few Baghdad officers spoke Arabic. They would arrive from places like Beijing and France speaking great Chinese or great French, which wasn't much help in Baghdad. Despite al Qaeda's rise in the 1990s as a terror group with global reach, the CIA had not emphasized Arabic language skills. A CIA clandestine officer told me that fewer than 10 percent of the CIA's 16,000 employees spoke a foreign language.

Despite its image, the CIA was not much attracted to danger. As violence in Iraq mounted, CIA officers only rarely left their protected station in the heavily secured Green Zone of Baghdad. When they did leave, they were accompanied by former special operations personnel as bodyguards. It is no surprise that the CIA has not penetrated the insurgent organizations in Iraq.

Officers were heard complaining about their assignment and about "Bush's war." They wanted out, despite the 25 percent increase in pay the Baghdad assignment carried. Few stayed more than six months. The station's institutional memory remained low. Army general George Casey, the top U.S. commander in Iraq, complained that CIA analytical reports were superficial, and that topics raised in the reports were not pursued.

There were some successes, however. The CIA was able to open six bases scattered around Iraq. Some pushed the military to kill Muqtada al-Sadr before the radical sheikh became too powerful. The military command refused, and al-Sadr went on to lead a deadly anti-U.S. revolt in 2006. The CIA had been right, but ignored.

By 2005, the lousy intelligence collection was the talk of the military. One example: the commander of the 160th Special Operations Aviation Regiment, the "Night Stalkers" who transport commandos to terror targets, convened a conference that fall in Tampa, home to U.S. Special Operations Command.

Special operators talked in a classroom-type setting about problems in Iraq. The chief criticism: the CIA could not often pinpoint the enemy. It gave operators a neighborhood when they needed an exact address.

That year, Army colonel Derek Harvey decided to explain the problem to the public. He wrote a paper intended for a service publication. Harvey is considered one of the military's leading experts on Iraq and its complex insurgency. He was an Iraq specialist at the Defense Intelligence Agency, then became an advisor to the Joint Chiefs of Staff. He would ultimately move with General David Petraeus to Iraq to brief him on the enemy. Anything Harvey wrote in 2005, in the Iraq war's third year, would surely get Washington's attention, especially that of members of Congress who were souring on the war and could not understand why the intelligence community could not locate top targets.

But General Petraeus, then commander of the U.S. Combined Arms Center at Fort Leavenworth, read Harvey's article and told him not to publish it. Too damning, the general said.

I obtained a copy, which can be read in its entirety in the Appendix. "Even after more than three years of conflict, we have yet to organize our intelligence assets efficiently and use our intelligence capability to best advantage," Harvey wrote. "The non-military national intelligence—FBI, Treasury, DIA, and CIA all-source efforts—are not doing enough to identify the networks that are moving foreign fighters/suicide bombers to Iraq, nor have they adequately identified the specific components of the insurgent networks within and external to Iraq, including key nodes, leadership, facilitators, bomb-makers, and financial support systems."

Other Harvey criticisms:

☐ "Unfortunately, Iraq is not the number-one priority for DIA and CIA, and has not been given priority resources."

☐ "The international terrorist increasingly looks at Iraq as the opportunity for what Clausewitz referred to as a 'battlefield' decision. Iraq for our adversaries is the central theater of confrontation with the West and its point of maximum effort, as is evidenced by the wide variety of foreign fighter recruits showing up among the insurgent forces."

☐ "To effectively counter this effort requires an intelligence structure that is at least as robust, flexible, rapid, and aggressive as the enemy.... Currently, the architecture has not been developed and adequate resources have not been provided."

☐ "A primary indicator of coalition deficiencies in intelligence assets and capabilities is starkly evident in the fact that tons of Iraqi Ba'ath Party documents, including intelligence service and terrorist liaison data from the previous regime, remain untranslated and unexploited. It is highly likely that these documents contain a veritable set of Rosetta Stones for understanding the key relationships of the current largely Sunni-driven insurgency."

☐ "We do not currently have a national-level 'center of excellence' that provides specific operational and strategic analytical focus on the insurgency leadership, organization, financing, and tactics (including IEDs), as well as comprehensive mapping of networked relations to global terrorist organizations."

A year after Harvey wrote his unpublished paper, his complaints were reinforced by the Iraq Study Group, a bipartisan panel appointed to give President Bush options on the deteriorating war in Iraq. Its report had a long list of intelligence failures in Iraq. In December 2006, the group, led by former secretary of state James Baker and former congressman Lee Hamilton, issued a blistering criticism of CIA and DIA work in Iraq. In essence, it sided not only with Harvey, but also with Porter Goss's House Intelligence Committee assessment of a troubled clandestine service.

"Our government still does not understand very well either the insurgency in Iraq or the role of the militias," said the commission's report. Intelligence agencies "are not doing enough to map the insurgency, dissect it, and understand it on a national and provincial level. The analytic community's knowledge of the organization, leadership, financing and operations of militias, as well as their relationship to government security forces, also falls far short of what policymakers need to know."

I asked Congressman Pete Hoekstra about intelligence shortfalls in Iraq. He said, "When I come back from Iraq, or even a briefing here, you learn how tough intelligence is. I don't walk out of there believing that I've got a crystal-clear picture of what the insurgency is, what the scope of it is, what the magnitude is, what the capabilities are. How much is international? How much is external? How much is al Qaeda? How much is Iranian? How much is Syrian? I walk out with lots of unanswered questions."

Yet Hoekstra is sympathetic, knowing how difficult it is to do anything in Iraq, much less walk out of the Green Zone and develop sources who can penetrate al Qaeda. "This is one of the things I do have an appreciation with the intelligence community on, is that the standard has been, the information you give us has to be as clear as two plus two is four. Anything less than that gold standard of giving us perfect information means that the intelligence is terrible. Sometimes I sense that policymakers believe if they get perfect information from intelligence, it gives them the answer as to what to do. That is not going to happen."

THE REVOLT

The two-month mark for the Goss regime in November 2004 proved to be the beginning of the end. He had already seen the Iraq shortfalls as House Intelligence Committee chairman. Goss delegated authority, especially when it came to transferring or firing personnel, and so his men made their moves. Pat Murray, the chief of staff, wanted to move the associate deputy director of clandestine service, Michael Sulick, to the CIA's station in New York at the UN ambassador's office. The idea was that if Goss was to reform the directorate of operations (later renamed the clandestine service), he had to break up the powerful duo of Sulick and his superior, deputy director Stephen Kappes. Sulick was one of the most respected men in the Agency. He had recruited some of the best Soviet spies during the Cold War from his Eastern European stations. If he resisted change, no change would happen.

Murray had sent Sulick an e-mail that the veteran case officer believed was insulting. When the men met to discuss his future, Sulick flipped a copy of the e-mail at Murray. "No Hill puke is going to tell me what to do," Sulick said. He retired rather than take the new assignment in his native New York. Kappes, another highly respected leader in the Agency—he had helped broker the 2002 deal with Libya's Muammar Gaddafi to get him to surrender his WMD program—quit in protest. Goss begged him to stay.

Their resignations were followed by the retirement of deputy director John McLaughlin, who had been passed over in favor of Goss as Tenet's replacement. Suddenly, the buzz in Langley was that Goss was cleaning house, although that wasn't the case. Division chiefs, figuring they were next, put in retirement papers. What started as a bid to reassign one senior manager took on the look of a massacre.

CIA insiders quickly leaked the retirements to the news media, which portrayed Goss's team as partisan Republicans who were ridding the CIA some of its finest staff members for purely political reasons.

On November 18, 2004, Goss issued what he thought was an anodyne message to employees. It read, in part: "CIA is, of course, a part of the executive branch primarily as a capabilities component. We do not make policy, though we do inform those who make it. We avoid political involvement, especially political partisanship."

The rank and file took those sentences as a veiled charge that Langley was a Democratic Party hotbed. But it was an ensuing paragraph that prompted another counter-attack, via the media. Goss said, "We support the administration and its policies in our work. As agency employees we do not identify with, support or champion opposition to the administration or its policies." The word *support* was interpreted by some as a demand to get in line and back Bush. Goss protested that "support" meant simply to supply information to policymakers so they could make policy. Nonetheless, insiders leaked the memo and spun it to reporters as a call to partisanship. The Agency had inflicted another wound on Goss.

Conservatives believed that Goss and Murray were trying to fix a broken agency that was sabotaging Bush's War on Terror. Senator John McCain, who served on the Robb-Silberman commission, came to Goss's defense. "I think this kind of shakeup is absolutely necessary," he told George Stephanopoulos on ABC's *This Week*. "George, the president appointed me to the weapons of mass destruction commission and one thing that has become abundantly clear, if it wasn't already: this is a dysfunctional agency and in some ways, a rogue agency.... We know very little more about North Korea and Iran than we did ten years ago. This agency needs to be reformed. And some of the actions of leaking information that could be damaging to the president prior to the election, using a compliant media, [were wrong,] if I may say so. Porter Goss is on the right track."

Bush was distressed by the intelligence leaks, and would complain about the CIA privately, though he refrained from criticizing it publicly. At a December 2006 press conference, after another leak, the president complained, "We've had a lot of leaks . . . as you know, some of them out of the—" He stopped short. If he named the CIA as his enemy, it would just generate "Bush at War with the CIA" stories and alienate the Agency. "I don't know where they're from," he quickly added.

Bush had sent Goss to Langley to reform the Agency, and when that caused a rebellion, he personally tried to quell it by paying the CIA a personal visit. He delivered an upbeat speech and then walked the halls of the analytical branch, greeting staff, back-slapping, and telling them they were all doing a great job.

Bush was certainly not anti-CIA. He announced a huge increase in the size of the clandestine service and gave Goss the pleasure of adding intelligence personnel as well as opening up stations and bases. Goss was guiding the CIA out of the Clinton retrenchment of 1990s and into a new century of expanding importance for America's intelligence services.

Unstated publicly was another big increase in funds. Congress was providing billions of dollars to establish a covert CIA presence in foreign countries, not in embassy stations or bases, but in phony commercial enterprises. Hundreds of CIA front companies, stocked with clandestine officers, sprang up in al Qaeda hotbeds like eastern Africa, the Middle East, and Pakistan.

The CIA was also adding to its reach. In early 2006, it became known that the Bush administration had approved the sale of six seaport operations to Dubai Ports World, owned by the United Arab Emirates. The UAE stood as one of America's staunchest Persian Gulf allies, home to a sprawling naval base where American warships docked and sailors disembarked for liberty among friendly Arabs. The United States sold the ruling emirs a wing of advanced F-16 strike bombers. Their unstated mission: penetrate Iran's airspace across the Gulf.

But the port deal stirred up a political storm. The UAE had played both sides. While hosting U.S. military forces, some of its emirs were courting the Afghanistan's Taliban and Osama bin Laden himself. The link came out in the 9-11 Commission's report. Democrats and Republicans complained that a country tied to Islamic militants should not be permitted to run America's ports, potential entry points for al Qaeda operatives and maybe for weapons of mass destruction.

What was not discussed, as a former senior Bush administration official told me, was that the UAE had decided to let the CIA place agents inside Dubai Ports World and its offices around the globe. The CIA considered this one of its post–September 11 coups. Dubai Ports World provided the Agency with the sort of non-embassy bases it badly needed. It also explains why the White House defended the deal so vigorously—until the political opposition grew so intense that the emirs decided to reverse the deal.

It was another defeat for Goss. But despite the turbulence within the Agency and the occasional setback in expanding the CIA's operations, Goss went before the Senate Armed Services Committee after five months on the job and said the CIA "is a special place. It's an organization of dedicated, patriotic people who are doing their best."

LEAKER

In the spring of 2006, all the things conservatives, Pete Hoekstra, and John McCain were saying about the CIA coalesced around a single CIA employee named Mary McCarthy. McCarthy was a longtime member of the clandestine service who had been shifted to the office of Langley's inspector general. Goss had asked the inspector general to find out who was leaking. The inspector general used interviews, analysis, and polygraphs to try to find leakers—and McCarthy was the first publicly known catch.

In April, Goss's team accused McCarthy of leaking information to the *Washington Post* about the Agency's secret holding cells in Eastern Europe. McCarthy was set to retire (ironically, to pursue a career in law), and her outing came in the same month the *Washington Post*'s series won the Pulitzer Prize. McCarthy's lawyer denied that she was the source.

But the Agency issued a hard-hitting statement saying she "knowingly and willfully shared classified intelligence" with reporters. McCarthy had served in the NSC under President Clinton from 1996 to 2001. Her NSC supervisor was Rand Beers, who resigned from the NSC in 2003 and joined the John

Kerry presidential campaign. When the CIA announced McCarthy's dismissal, she asked Beers to vouch for her.

But as reporters investigated McCarthy, suspicions rose among CIA critics that a Kerry operative was working inside the CIA and leaking stories to Washington's liberal media establishment. McCarthy, as it turned out, was another Kerry campaign contributor. She had contributed the maximum under federal law of $2,000 in March 2004, and then $5,000 to the Democratic Party of Ohio, the state that would decide the election. She also gave $500 to the Democratic National Committee. Her husband added $2,000 to the Kerry bid and $500 for the reelection of Democratic senator Barbara Mikulski of Maryland. Federal Election Commission records do not show any McCarthy contributions to Republicans.

"NEGROPONTE STABBED ME IN THE BACK"

Goss was the second-highest-ranking intelligence figure in the administration. Above him was John Negroponte. Negroponte, a career diplomat, had been America's ambassador to Iraq when Bush tapped him to become the first director of national intelligence. The Negroponte-Goss relationship should have clicked. It did not. They had been Yale fraternity brothers in Psi Upsilon. Goss went off in the 1960s to become a CIA officer in Latin America while Negroponte, himself an ardent foe of communism, joined the Foreign Service.

But this seemingly perfect pairing was a mismatch. Goss went out of his way to praise Negroponte. At one Defense Department appearance, Goss spoke first. Negroponte, he said, was the right man, appointed at the right time, to oversee the community's sixteen intelligence agencies. When Negroponte spoke, he ignored Goss. "The reaching out all came from one side," an aide said later. "He [Negroponte] maintained a regal manner."

The stylistic differences then gave way to deep disagreements. Goss wanted the CIA to do all the things listed in the 1947 National Security Act that created it. But the directorate of national intelligence (DNI) had other ideas. Though the CIA operated the Counterterrorism Center, the DNI set up its own National Counterterrorism Center, just down the road from Langley in Tyson's Corner, Virginia. Goss accepted that. But then the DNI started staffing it with the CIA's best analysts. "He keeps pushing. He wants all my people," Goss complained. Moreover, it was Goss's belief that analysts and operators should work under the same roof, share information, and interact, while Negroponte's separate center seemed to be an attempt to cut the CIA out.

Goss had thought the DNI was supposed to provide budget oversight and guidance. But Negroponte's staff started micromanaging the clandestine service, issuing orders and coming up with ideas for operations.

Negroponte also pressed Goss to get rid of a close aide, executive director Kyle "Dusty" Foggo. The CIA inspector general had opened a probe of Foggo and his ties to two defense contractors. Goss resisted the firing, arguing that Foggo had not been charged. Foggo eventually quit and was later indicted.

By the winter of 2006, Goss had grown tired. He complained in a press interview about his grueling schedule. The president wanted Goss to brief him at 6:30 a.m. (just as Tenet had done). The appointment meant Goss had to get up well before dawn and get briefed himself. Sometimes the ceremony took place at an intercept-proof room in Goss's Northern Virginia home. Other times, he took his limo first to Langley and then to the White House.

But lack of sleep was only one problem. At a closed Senate Intelligence Committee hearing, he confessed he still did not control the CIA bureaucracy after more than a year on the job. Staff members exchanged glances in disbelief. It seemed a confession that he was not up to the task.

In May 2006, Josh Bolten, the White House chief of staff, telephoned Goss and asked for his resignation. Always the good Republican soldier, Goss hurried to the Oval Office for his farewell to the president. Goss was in a chair, next to the president, when the press was let in. The two shook hands.

"He's instilled a sense of professionalism," Bush said about Goss's performance at the CIA.

Goss spoke briefly. "I honestly believe that we have improved dramatically your goals for our nation's intelligence capabilities," he said. Bush ended it with a "God bless." Negroponte sat a few feet away on a couch, alone. Goss later told friends, "Negroponte stabbed me in the back."

President Bush had sent Goss—his fellow elected Republican and fellow private school and Yale alumnus—to Langley to get the Agency in order and make sure it danced to the White House's tune. When Goss walked away from Langley, after months of bureaucratic combat, he had barely left a mark on the CIA.

ENTER GENERAL HAYDEN

Bush picked as Goss's replacement Air Force general Michael Hayden, a career intelligence specialist who ran the National Security Agency and had also worked in the DNI. One of Hayden's first acts was to woo CIA veteran Stephen Kappes back to the Agency and make him deputy director. Hayden also reached out to the *Washington Post* with an exclusive interview and granted interviews to other major press outlets. He was determined to win over the mainstream media.

He was also determined to stop the leaks by raising morale at Langley. He began an open e-mail system. Workers sent him hundreds of messages, and he reciprocated, updating the entire CIA workforce on his trips and meetings. He also told them the importance of not pushing agendas in the news media.

Hayden felt proud enough about his open-house style that he told C-SPAN's Brian Lamb in an April 2007 interview that he had plugged the holes.

"You may recall, in my confirmation hearing I talked about getting CIA out of the press as source or subject," the director said. "And I did that, because the preceding twelve months it was almost daily that the agency was in the paper and very often being criticized, and very often being criticized unfairly."

Former CIA deputy director John McLaughlin had denied, in a *Washington Post* op-ed, that the CIA had been leaking to the press. In November 2004, the same month his resignation was announced, McLaughlin had written: "It is alleged that the CIA was leaking material before the election to damage the president.... There were leaks, to be sure, but the truth is that no one, other than those who leaked and those who reported, knows where they were actually coming from. What I do know beyond a doubt is that the CIA was not institutionally plotting against the president, as some allege. The accusation is absurd. CIA officers are career professionals who work for the president."

But in April 2007, Hayden was at least tacitly acknowledging that the CIA had, in fact, leaked.

Hayden also provided Lamb with a string of statistics that underscored just how damaging the Clinton years had been to the CIA. One-fifth of the CIA's analysts and one-seventh of its total number of employees had been hired in the past twelve months. In fact, half of the entire agency had been hired since September 11.

Congressman Hoekstra, the ranking Republican on the House Intelligence Committee, thought Hayden's C-SPAN appearance was a lot of happy talk focused on winning over Washington's press corps with nothing said about demanding accountability and results from the CIA. Just the month before, in March 2007, Hoekstra had sent a private letter to national security advisor Stephen Hadley about a trip he had made to the Middle East and North Africa, inspecting firsthand the CIA stations there. His conclusion: five years after September 11, nothing had changed. CIA officers in the Riyadh station in Saudi Arabia were year-long ticket punchers and received two months off during that single year. If one subtracts that vacation time, plus the six months it takes to get accustomed in-country, that left only four productive months.

Hoekstra was also appalled that these most important anti-terrorist stations were staffed by so many employees in their twenties with little experience. "I think you would be personally troubled by the extraordinarily young workforce we are sending out to the field," Hoekstra told Hadley. "I understand better than most what the Clinton administration personnel at the CIA did to our human capital capabilities and I fully appreciate what the president has directed to begin recovering from those cuts. However, you need to know that far too many of our officers serving in this critical region are on either only their first or second tours of duty. Although perhaps unavoidable because of the limited numbers, we are sending 'green' inexperienced personnel to do some of America's most demanding work."

Between the careerism of so many older employees and the years of Clinton cuts, there was little alternative to hoping that a new generation of field officers would do a better job. But it is a sad commentary on the intelligence capabilities of America's premier intelligence service. And as Porter Goss learned, the prevailing sentiment at Langley is that things are just dandy the way they are.

CHAPTER 6

THE WILSONS

"The ambassador's trip .... had been authorized at a low level within the CPD, the counter-proliferation division of the directorate of operations at the CIA, and had produced such inconclusive results that the press office had trouble finding people who remembered the details of the trip .... The mission had not been undertaken at the vice president's behest, and the vice president was never briefed on the trip's less-than-compelling results."

Former CIA director George Tenet, At the Center of the Storm

John Dion, who runs the Justice Department's counter-espionage section, reviews scores of criminal referrals each year from the CIA. When secrets are exposed in the press, the Agency is required by law to contact Justice. Not every exposed secret merits a referral, though, and few referrals lead to leak investigations. If Justice launched a criminal investigation based on every referral, it would need to hire hundreds more lawyers.

The process is a bit subjective; it's up to the CIA to begin it. It is one of Langley's most powerful tools, and Washington politicians know it, because senators and congressman, by intent or inadvertently, sometimes discuss classified information in public. Right after the September 11 attacks, Senator

Orrin Hatch disclosed classified evidence against al Qaeda he had just learned from the CIA. He later apologized. No one wants to be the subject of a criminal referral.

In July 2003, Dion reviewed one of about a hundred referrals he got each year. No bells went off. It did not appear to be an issue of grave national security. The CIA said one of its clandestine officers, Valerie Plame, had been named in a July 14, 2003, column by Robert Novak, an old Washington hand who mixes reporting with opinion. The Novak column centered on Plame's husband, Joseph Wilson, and his trip to Niger to investigate claims of Saddam Hussein approaching that country to buy uranium. Wilson had written a now-famous op-ed in the *New York Times* that month revealing his secret mission. He said he found no evidence that Saddam had tried to buy uranium and said his mission rebutted a key line in President Bush's State of the Union address—the controversial "sixteen words."

But why would the administration send a former ambassador like Wilson to do intelligence work? Novak's column told why: it quoted administration sources as saying his wife got him the job. Novak found her maiden name, Valerie Plame, in Wilson's *Who's Who* entry and mentioned her in his column.

The CIA cried foul. The Agency's general counsel office typed up a referral explaining what is termed an "unauthorized disclosure" under executive order 12333. The counsel informed George Tenet that the referral was headed to the Department of Justice. An Agency director has never stopped the process, but, in a sense, Tenet was tacitly approving an investigation of the White House.

The paperwork said the item may have violated the Intelligence Identities Protection Act. Dion looked the referral over. His office sent the CIA an eleven-point questionnaire, as is routine. (The questionnaire can be found in the Appendix.) One question was what effect the disclosure would have on national security. A Justice source told me the CIA made a weak case that the unauthorized release of Plame's identity damaged national security. (In contrast, a subsequent leak from the CIA to the *New York Times* about the terrorist surveillance program did trigger an immediate criminal probe.) And it was unclear whether Plame qualified under the protection act, as she worked under "non-official cover." She had traveled overseas in the guise of an employee of a marketing firm. Non-official cover is different than "official cover," which usually means the CIA officer is assigned to an embassy, and the host government is notified.

Dion, a career prosecutor at Justice for more than thirty years, under Democratic and Republican presidents, took no action on the CIA referral. He had no plans to start a formal investigation, a Justice source told me. The referral seemed so weak that the office of Attorney General John Ashcroft was not informed.

But then the CIA leaked the story. On the evening of September 23, two months after the referral, MSNBC broke the news. The CIA had sent a criminal referral to the Justice Department in the Plame affair. The media and political pressure grew intense. Before he went home that Friday, Dion decided to make the Novak column a criminal case.

Justice officials are certain that only the CIA could have executed the leak to the media. Only Dion and a few others in his section knew of it. These people are perhaps the most-tight-lipped in government, because of the extremely sensitive matters they handle. "I never talk to reporters," Dion once told a colleague. Once, at a Justice reception, a network news reporter introduced herself. Dion said, "Nice to meet you," and then walked away. Justice officials also noted the leak came as the public learned that investigators had not found WMD in Iraq, making the CIA's intelligence wrong again.

Less than a week later, a news report based on one anonymous source implicated two White House aides, who had allegedly leaked Plame's identity in order to ruin her career—as revenge against Wilson for his criticism of President Bush. The Novak column was part of a White House conspiracy, Democrats charged. They demanded an independent investigator.

At the end of 2003, Justice turned the probe over to Patrick Fitzgerald, a career prosecutor serving as the U.S. attorney in Chicago. Fitzgerald quickly made a decision with far-reaching consequences for Washington's power players. Normally, it is up to the attorney general to approve any subpoena directed at a news reporter. Such action is rarely taken, and the Justice Department had guidelines in place against the subpoena of reporters. The Bush Justice Department approved only one: for the phone records of two *New York Times* reporters whose story, prosecutors say, tipped off an Islamic charity to an upcoming raid. Fitzgerald decided that as the issue was who in the administration had leaked Plame's identity, he and he alone, not the administration, would decide on press subpoenas.

Fitzgerald's investigation suddenly ballooned into one of the most expansive criminal investigations of the White House since Watergate and Monica Lewinsky—all because the CIA leaked a referral that the Justice Department thought too inconsequential to merit investigation. Critics predicted Bush's doom, with top aides certain to go to jail.

THE SCANDAL BEGINS

Fitzgerald's probe focused on the office of Vice President Dick Cheney. In early 2002, the vice president had made a special request to CIA headquarters. He did not know it then, but the request would plunge President Bush into a political crisis.

The Bush administration by this time had ousted the Taliban in Afghanistan and laid the markers for a global war against al Qaeda. The Pentagon had established a presence for special operations forces in Yemen, the Horn of Africa, and the Philippines. Now attention turned to Iraq. Bush had decided, unofficially, to take out Saddam Hussein, ending the chance his weapons would fall into the hands of al Qaeda. In making the case for removing Saddam, the administration wanted to know about Iraq's relationship

with the impoverished African nation of Niger. Saddam had purchased yellowcake, a refined uranium used in making nuclear bombs, from Niger in the
early 1980s. (U.S. troops would find some in Iraq when they invaded in
2003.) The question was whether he had purchased more.

Cheney was told by the Defense Intelligence Agency of Italian reports indicating that Baghdad had contracted with Niger to buy five hundred tons of
yellowcake. In other words, Saddam wanted to build bombs again after Operation Desert Storm virtually wiped out his matured nuclear weapons program. If true, it all but made the case for forcibly removing Saddam from
power. The White House would learn only belatedly that the reports were
based on forged documents. They were also relying on the fact that the
British had separate reports of a Niger-Iraq connection.

Cheney had had a rocky relationship with the CIA ever since the September 11 attacks. Cheney was perhaps the president's closest advisor, and as a
former secretary of defense, he was especially focused on national security.
To properly advise the president, he felt he needed firsthand knowledge of
what the intelligence community knew about al Qaeda, Saddam Hussein,
radical Islam, and other topics. He began visiting Langley for briefings. Some
in the CIA regarded this as too much oversight, and soon stories started
appearing in the news media that the vice president's visits amounted to
political pressure to produce analysis he wanted.

Here is what the *Washington Post* reported: "Vice President Cheney and
his most senior aide made multiple trips to the CIA over the past year to
question analysts studying Iraq's weapons programs and alleged links to al
Qaeda, creating an environment in which some analysts felt they were being
pressured to make their assessments fit with the Bush administration's policy objectives, according to senior intelligence officials."

The Senate Intelligence Committee investigated this charge in 2004, and
senators were told by CIA analysts that Cheney in fact had not pressured

them. The final bipartisan report quoted one of Cheney's CIA briefers as saying, "There was no attempt to get us to hew to a particular point of view ourselves or to come to a certain conclusion. It was trying to figure out, why do we come to this conclusion." Two years after the "pressure charges" circulated in the media, the committee found them baseless. But Cheney stood bloodied in 2002. He had dared to probe CIA findings, and got burned.

"In terms of asking questions, I plead guilty," Cheney told Tim Russert on *Meet the Press*. "I ask a hell of a lot of questions. That's my job."

JOE WILSON

Cheney's visits coincided with his request that the Niger story be checked out. That request found its way to the director of operation's counter-proliferation office, the unit where Valerie Plame worked. Though Cheney had not asked for an investigator to be sent to Niger, within days, a curious choice was made. Former ambassador Joe Wilson was summoned from retirement and sent to the African country to investigate.

Wilson had gained momentary fame in 1990 as the senior diplomat in Baghdad in the walk-up to Desert Storm. By all accounts he was courageous in standing up to Saddam, and he won kudos from the media and President George H. W. Bush. But his Foreign Service career did not take off. When Wilson finally won an ambassadorship a year after Desert Storm, it was to the tiny African nation of Gabon, not a country high on the list of ambitious diplomats. He retired in 1998 and became a consultant.

Wilson had little or no experience as an intelligence investigator, and was politically opposed to President Bush (he had donated money to Al Gore's 2000 presidential campaign and eventually became an advisor to John Kerry's campaign). Nonetheless, he was off on a secret mission to Niger to investigate one of the most important prewar questions facing the Bush administration. In Niger, over sweet mint tea, Wilson interviewed some of his old contacts (he had worked at the American embassy in Niger from 1976 to

1978) and upon his return to the U.S. filed an oral report at Langley, which disseminated a written assessment.

In Bush's January 2003 State of the Union address two months before the invasion of Iraq, the president said the famous "sixteen words": "The British government has learned that Saddam Hussein recently sought significant quantities of uranium from Africa." In May, two months after the invasion, U.S. inspectors had not found any weapons of mass destruction. As the media scrambled to explain why, *New York Times* columnist Nicholas D. Kristof wrote of a former U.S. ambassador who had gone to Niger and found no evidence of a Baghdad bid to buy yellowcake. Two months later, on July 6, 2003, Wilson revealed himself as the former ambassador in question in a *Times* op-ed, "What I Didn't Find in Africa." He said he was informed in February by the CIA that Cheney wanted an investigation and "the agency officials asked if I would travel to Niger.... The vice president's office asked a serious question. I was asked to help formulate the answer." Wilson concluded, according to his op-ed, that no uranium transaction had taken place.

The column left the impression, to some, that Wilson was Cheney's man, which made the embarrassment to Cheney all the greater. Wilson instantly became a hero to the Left and the media, who made fresh charges that Bush had misled the country. But Wilson's column did not, in fact, disprove what Bush said. The president did not talk of a completed transaction, but of an attempted transaction.

A week later, the Niger affair blew up into a scandal that would stalk the White House for three years. Conservative columnist Novak, a dogged reporter just as likely to skewer Republicans as Democrats (and who had opposed the invasion of Iraq from the beginning), wrote his "Mission to Niger" column. The CIA sought a criminal probe, and leaked its request. Then, on September 28, 2003, the *Washington Post* published a story that would reverberate through Washington and the media, taking the scandal to new heights. The *Post* quoted a "senior administration official" as saying two

White House officials had "called at least six Washington journalists and disclosed the identify and occupation of Wilson's wife." It was "meant purely and simply for revenge," the source said.

Other journalists accepted this story—that the White House had launched an orchestrated campaign against Wilson and his wife—as gospel. "The administration tried to bait at least six reporters with its nefarious story, but only Novak bit," wrote Eric Alterman in the leftist *Nation* magazine. "This conspiracy clearly reaches into the highest levels of our government," wrote Tom Matzzie, Washington director of the anti-Bush MoveOn.org. "This could be among the worst presidential scandals in our history."

Wilson himself cited the *Post* story to fan the flames. "In my judgment... after having read the *Washington Post* article, which quotes a source as saying that there were an initial two officials who contacted six journalists, my thinking on this is there were probably two waves," he told Tim Russert on *Meet the Press*. "There was the potential crime of leaking my wife's name by these two officers to six journalists." The *Post* later published a story crediting itself with influencing the Justice Department to start an investigation, which began when Justice named Fitzgerald as special counsel on December 30, 2003.

Wilson, meanwhile, continued to hurl accusations at the White House, wrote a bestselling book blaming the Bush administration for outing his wife, and became a regular on cable news and the lecture circuit. Wilson told at least one audience, "At the end of the day, it's of keen interest to me to see whether or not we can get Karl Rove frog-marched out of the White House in handcuffs."

Cheered on by the liberal press, Fitzgerald sent out FBI investigators, subpoenaed e-mails and telephone records, and summoned reporters and White House officials to the grand jury. He threatened reporters with jail if they did not reveal their confidential sources. One, Judith Miller of the *New York Times*, went to jail for eighty-five days. For reporters who believed in protecting the confidentiality of their sources, Fitzgerald was setting a horrible precedent. But because his ultimate target was the Bush White House, the mainstream media continued to give him lavish and positive coverage. Rove went before the grand jury several times. The press all but predicted his indictment in front-page stories.

FIZZLE

But three years later, the Plame affair fizzled. Fitzgerald sought no indictment against Rove or against any White House official for leaking Plame's identity. The lone indictment came against I. Lewis "Scooter" Libby, Cheney's chief of staff, on charges of lying to the grand jury and the FBI about who first told him that Plame worked for the CIA.

From independent inquiries and the accounts of subpoenaed journalists, we know the scandal was much pettier than it seemed.

Plame's role

A 2004 Senate Intelligence Committee bipartisan report on prewar intelligence documented for the first time Plame's role in her husband's mission. She had denied that she recommended her husband, but the committee turned up a memo she wrote suggesting him just a day before he got the job.

This is the most crucial piece of evidence in the entire episode. Why? Because it explains why Bush administration officials were talking about Plame once Wilson leaked his mission to Nicholas Kristof at the *New York Times*. The CIA bureaucracy did not inform either George Tenet or Vice President Cheney that Wilson was sent on such an important trip. Blindsided by the Kristof column, the White House made inquiries as to how it happened. The CIA reported back that Plame, not Tenet, had suggested Wilson for the job. There is no evidence the CIA informed Cheney's office that she was covert.

When Wilson seemingly implied in his *New York Times* column that Cheney had sent him to Niger, a few administration officials wanted to disabuse reporters of this falsehood. They told what they knew to be the truth—that Plame, not Cheney, had recommended Wilson go to Niger. The Wilsons still deny this. They have to; if they were to acknowledge it, they would forfeit their pending federal lawsuit.

Democrats, too, realize the importance of Plame's role. Even after Senate Intelligence Committee staffers turned up the Plame memo and a CIA colleague said Plame had "offered up" Wilson's name, Democrats prevented the report from concluding that Plame had recommended Wilson for the Niger investigation. So Intelligence Committee chairman Pat Roberts wrote it into his addendum.

No smear campaign

We know today from the journalists who went before the grand jury that they had contacted the White House about the Wilson trip, not the other way around. The reporters were syndicated columnist Robert Novak; Judith Miller, then of the *New York Times*; Matthew Cooper, then of *Time* magazine; and Bob Woodward of the *Washington Post*.

Novak told the grand jury that his original source was deputy secretary of state Richard Armitage. Woodward said he asked Armitage in an interview at his office at the State Department why the CIA would send someone like Wilson to Niger. Armitage answered that he had heard that Wilson's wife got him the job. Novak later telephoned Rove, raised the question of the Niger trip, and mentioned the wife angle. "You know that too," Rove responded. Novak said he found her name in Joseph Wilson's *Who's Who* listing.

Matthew Cooper said he called Rove after Wilson's July 6 op-ed appeared in the *New York Times*. He said Rove discounted Wilson's findings, explaining his wife recommended him. Rove did not mention her name. The call lasted two minutes.

Judith Miller told the grand jury she initiated a discussion with Scooter Libby over why no weapons of mass destruction had been found in Iraq. In two subsequent interviews, Libby criticized the Wilson report as incomplete and mentioned Wilson's wife briefly, without saying her name. Bob Woodward said he heard of Wilson's wife from Armitage. Woodward characterized the discussion as "gossip."

Ari Fleischer, Bush's press secretary at the time, testified at Libby's trial that he had learned of Plame's role from Libby. He remembered passing it on to a few reporters who contacted him. Fleischer's story, however, was in dispute. One reporter said he never had such a discussion. Fleischer denied such a discussion with another reporter, who recalled otherwise.

Taken collectively, the reporters' statements show a consistent pattern. They contacted White House officials, asked about the Wilson trip, and received vague answers about Wilson's wife. It is true that before the White House officials said anything they should have learned Plame's status at the CIA and then declined to comment. But an orchestrated smear the Plame Affair is not. At worst, a few White House officials gave reporters what they believed to be the truth about who had chosen Wilson to go to Niger: it wasn't Dick Cheney, it was Wilson's wife.

When the *Washington Post* reported that two White House officials had telephoned six reporters to out Plame, the paper, according to all the evidence, got it wrong. This is not a criticism of the *Post*, but of its source. The source worked inside the White House press operation. A reporter would rationally conclude he was in a position to know.

Wilson's statements

The Senate inquiry also discovered that Wilson's *New York Times* op-ed had left out an important fact. Wilson might not have found evidence of a completed transaction for yellowcake, but he did turn up evidence that Saddam's regime had made a commercial overture to Niger. The former prime minister of Niger told Wilson that he had met with an Iraqi delegation in 1999 to discuss "expanding commercial relations," according to a subsequent 2005 report by the bipartisan Robb-Silberman commission. The prime minister interpreted this as an inquiry about yellowcake: the only exportable product Niger had that was of interest to Iraq. He did not pursue it because he did not want to violate UN sanctions.

This was evidence that Iraq still sought yellowcake, even if it had not succeeded in buying it from Niger. Senator Pat Roberts's addendum took note of Wilson's many allegations against Bush and Cheney. "In an interview with the committee staff, Mr. Wilson was asked how he knew some of the things he was stating publicly with such confidence," Roberts wrote. "On at least three occasions, he admitted that he had no direct knowledge to support some of his claims and that he was drawing on either unrelated past experiences or no information at all. . . . The former ambassador, either by design or through ignorance, gave the American people and, for that matter, the world a version of events that was inaccurate, unsubstantiated, and misleading."

Wilson said on *Meet the Press* that when he went to the CIA to discuss the mission, his wife was not there. "I can tell you that when the decision was made, which was made after a briefing and after a gaming out at the Agency with the intelligence community, there was nobody in the room when we went through this that I knew."

The Senate report tells a different story. It says Plame, in fact, attended the meeting. An attendee's notes state the meeting was "apparently convened by [Plame] who had the idea to dispatch [Wilson] to use his contacts to sort out the Iraq-Niger uranium issue." Plame told the committee staff she was just there to introduce her husband and then left.

Wilson also told the committee that he was the unnamed source for a *Washington Post* story saying that the documents showing a yellowcake deal between Iraq and Niger (provided by an Italian journalist) were forged. Pressed by committee staff, Wilson acknowledged he had never reviewed the documents or CIA reports on them.

Wilson had demanded the CIA not disclose that he had worked for the Agency. Yet in his *Times* op-ed, he wrote, "There was nothing secret or earth-shattering in my report, just as there was nothing secret about my trip."

Finally, Wilson told reporters that Vice President Cheney was briefed on his report before the president's State of the Union address. The Senate report said Cheney was not briefed on Wilson's trip before the speech.

The bottom line is that when Vice President Cheney requested a CIA investigation into Iraq's dealings with Niger, the proper response would have been for George Tenet to follow up and decide how to proceed. If he had, there would have been no Wilson trip and no scandal.

The Plame-Niger affair revealed again how the CIA, through incompetence and cunning, did a disservice to the war. A small cadre of officers named Wilson as chief investigator, but never told the vice president about it, nor briefed him on the former ambassador's findings before Wilson went public. The documents obtained by Italian intelligence turned out to be blatant forgeries. The CIA had copies of the documents but did not examine them. The 2005 bipartisan Robb-Silberman commission on intelligence and weapons of mass destruction later called the lack of review "a major failure of the intelligence system."

Did Iraq seek yellowcake in Niger? The 2004 Senate Intelligence Committee report concluded there was insufficient evidence to prove that Saddam sought uranium from Africa. But the British government reexamined its own intelligence and concluded that Saddam Hussein's regime had, indeed, tried to obtain yellowcake.

It also needs to be mentioned that while the *Washington Post* gave extensive and sympathetic coverage to the Wilsons, the paper's editorial board came to a different conclusion about the former ambassador in September 2006. The *Post*'s editorial page said:

Far too much attention and debate in Washington has been devoted to [Plame's] story and that of her husband. It follows that one of the most sensational charges leveled against the Bush White House— that it orchestrated the leak of Ms. Plame's identity to ruin her career and thus punish Mr. Wilson—is untrue.... It now appears that the person most responsible for the end of Ms. Plame's CIA career is Mr. Wilson. Mr. Wilson chose to go public with an explosive charge, claiming—falsely, as it turned out—that he had debunked reports of Iraqi uranium-shopping in Niger and that his report had circulated to senior administration officials. He ought to have expected that both those officials and journalists such as Mr. Novak would ask why a retired ambassador would have been sent on such a mission and that the answer would point to his wife.... It's unfortunate that so many people took him seriously.

It's also unfortunate that this entire media and legal circus, and the untold hours it occupied the White House during a time of war, was the result of the September 2003 CIA leak of the case's referral to the Justice Department— all to work against the Bush administration.

PLAME'S NEW STORY

On a rainy Friday in March 2007, Valerie Plame chose to speak to the House Committee on Oversight and Government Reform, a committee that claimed jurisdiction over virtually every aspect of the Bush administration. The Republican loss in November had handed the committee gavel to Henry Waxman, a highly partisan liberal Democrat from California. Waxman positioned the panel as a venue to embarrass the administration by holding hearings on Iraq and inviting Plame to testify.

Scooter Libby had been convicted earlier that month of perjury and obstruction of justice. No one was charged with leaking Valerie Plame's name, which had been the whole purpose of the original criminal probe. A CIA officer, Robert Grenier, had testified that Plame had recommended Wilson for the Niger investigation. And as the *Post* editorial board concluded, the person most responsible for ending Valerie Plame's career at the CIA was her husband. The Plame story should have been over. But Waxman hoped he could keep it going.

Testifying under oath, Plame told Waxman's panel that she had not recommended her husband for the Niger mission. She said an officer in her division, a woman, had received a call from the vice president's office about investigating the Niger connection. She described the woman as "very upset." She testified that another officer, a male, "passed by" at that moment and suggested sending her husband to Niger. She said that she went with her male colleague to her division chief and that her colleague recommended Wilson. "The supervisor then asked me to send an e-mail to the counter-proliferation division chief letting him know that this was— might happen," she testified. This is the e-mail, allegedly, that was quoted by the Senate Intelligence Committee in 2004.

But Plame's testimony was a break with her previous testimony to the Senate Intelligence Committee. She had not mentioned a male colleague in her secret deposition. "This is a whole new story," said Senate Intelligence Committee vice chairman Christopher "Kit" Bond, a Missouri Republican.

Plame's public testimony that she did not recommend her husband for the trip prompted Bond to address the issue again in a May 2007 committee report. He inserted Plame's February 12, 2002, memo to her boss. She wrote about the Niger investigation and then wrote, "My husband is willing to help if it makes sense, but no problem if not." She added that Wilson "may be in a position to assist."

The Senate Intelligence Committee's 2004 report, as we've seen, quoted a Plame colleague as saying she "offered up his name." A Republican source told me Plame had testified then that she could not remember how her husband's name came up.

Plame also told Waxman's House committee, "My role in this was to go home that night, without revealing any classified information, of course, and ask my husband would he be willing to come into CIA headquarters the following week and talk to the people there. At that meeting, I introduced him, and I left."

Of the vice president's request for information on Iraq's interest in Niger's uranium, she testified to the House committee, "It was a serious question . . . and it deserved a serious answer." But she told the Senate Intelligence Committee that she told her husband, "There's this crazy report."

Questioned by Congressman Tom Davis, a Virginia Republican, Plame acknowledged that she was there when Wilson first leaked the existence of his trip to *New York Times* columnist Nicholas Kristof at breakfast in Washington.

"Was any of the information classified, to your knowledge?" Davis asked.

"Not that I'm aware of," she answered. But it was Wilson himself who had asked that the CIA keep his trip secret, and Plame made no attempt to stop her husband from disclosing it. If she had been concerned about protecting her identity as a CIA employee, why was she at a breakfast where her husband told a reporter that he had been sent by the CIA to Niger? The breakfast, interestingly, came the day after she and her husband attended a conference of the Senate Democratic Policy Committee.

Asked about posing with her husband in a flamboyant photograph for *Vanity Fair* magazine when she was still covert, she said, "Having lived most of my life very much under the radar, my learning curve was steep, and it was more trouble than it was worth." According to the *New York Times*, Plame also signed a multi-million-dollar book deal.

As the husband of someone in the clandestine service, Wilson was expected to help his wife stay anonymous. Writing a *New York Times* column about his trip to Niger fell far short of honoring that tradition, as did posing for *Vanity Fair* and writing a book.

In 1999, the Senate Intelligence Committee did a secret study of how well the CIA protects the identifies of undercover officers. It gave the CIA a failing grade. Plame was not in the study, but she could have been. She worked at CIA headquarters and drove there from her home. It would take a foreign agent exactly one day to follow her to Langley and then learn her identity through public records, just as Novak did.

The Wilsons, in their lawsuit against Cheney and others, are represented by Melanie Sloan. She runs Citizens for Responsibility and Ethics in Washington, a "non-partisan" litigation and pressure group, and is a former legal staffer for two of Washington's most liberal anti-Bush members of Congress, Democrats John Conyers of Michigan and Charles Schumer of New York. She did not respond to requests to be interviewed for this book.

A few days after the hearing, Robert Novak wrote a biting column about the proceedings. He zeroed in on someone who hadn't been there in person, but whose behind-the-scenes maneuvering had aided chairman Henry Waxman. CIA director Michael Hayden had met with Waxman and Intelligence Committee chairman Silvestre Reyes before the hearing—but not with Republicans Tom Davis or Pete Hoekstra. Hayden had helped Waxman craft a statement on Plame's covert status. In his column, Novak pointed out that Hoekstra had been trying, with no luck, to get the CIA to provide him the same information. Novak surmised that Hayden was jockeying for the job of intelligence czar in the next Democratic administration.

Hayden fumed over the column and telephoned Hoekstra, whom Novak had mentioned.

"How can you say these things, Pete?" Hayden asked the congressman.

"Hey, Mike, all I know is you went and met with Silvestre Reyes and with Waxman before the hearing. You gave them a bunch of talking points. You didn't meet with the Republicans. Supposedly you sent the talking points to us as quickly as possible but I never received them. Henry Waxman sure had all the talking points at the hearing specifically from Mike Hayden. You helped prepare the Democrats for the hearing."

"We made sure that we faxed this stuff to you," Hayden protested. Hoekstra said no one could find it.

Days later, the spat moved to an unlikely venue: the annual Gridiron Club Dinner. Washington's power elite look forward to the tux-and-tails soirée as a night of uncustomary burlesque in a usually buttoned-down city. Journalists and government honchos stage comedic skits that can take the edge off a war or rejuvenate an image. The town still talks about Nancy Reagan softening her royal aura by singing "Secondhand Clothes" at the 1982 dinner.

Victoria Toensing, a leading Republican attorney in Washington, spotted Hayden sitting with Veterans Affairs secretary Jim Nicholson. The night before, at a dinner party at Novak's home, Toensing had complained to Nicholson about Hayden's statement to Waxman. She had testified at the hearing that Plame was not covered under the Intelligence Protection Identities Act, and assumed Nicholson had conveyed her complaints to his dinner partner.

Toensing, who had helped draft the original Intelligence Protection Identities Act, walked over to Hayden's table and bluntly told him, "You don't know the law." Hayden defended his position that Plame was classified.

Toensing returned her table, where her guests, including Pete Hoekstra, were sitting. Hayden followed her and, in his dress blues, kneeled down to face Hoekstra.

"I know you guys are talking about me," Hayden said.

"Don't flatter yourself," Hoekstra said. "We're enjoying the Gridiron. This is a night of just fun. Lighthearted entertainment and all that. We're not talking about serious business. And if we were talking about serious business, I wouldn't even assume you're the top of mind for me and Victoria tonight."

Hayden walked away. CIA spokesman Mark Mansfield declined to comment on events at the dinner except to say, "Anyone who knows Director Hayden knows he is a straight shooter."

ARMITAGE'S FAILURES

To the Rove camp, there were two villains in the Plame fiasco: the CIA and Richard Armitage. The CIA leaked. Armitage kept quiet.

Not only did someone at the CIA leak information about the referral, which was lying dormant at the Justice Department, but then the CIA also did not inform the administration that Plame was undercover when it told the White House how Wilson was chosen for the trip. The CIA director, by law, is required to protect sources and methods. He should have alerted the White House that Plame was a covert employee.

Once a criminal probe began in September 2003, deputy secretary of state Richard Armitage realized his remark to Novak had started it all. He testified to prosecutors, but never informed the public or the White House. If he had, Washington would have seen that the whole affair began with an offhand remark from someone who was not happy with Bush administration policy and not particularly close to either Rove or Cheney. But Armitage remained silent. He explained later that special counsel Patrick Fitzgerald had warned him not to talk. But Mark Corallo, a former Justice Department spokesman who was later hired by Rove as a consultant, said Justice prosecutors did not gag Armitage.

"All he had to do was walk into the president's office and say, 'It was me,'" Corallo told me. "The whole thing would have been over. I know why he didn't. He was against the [Iraq] war. He didn't like Cheney. He's a coward to have put people through this thing that could ruin their lives. This is the guy who refused to do the right thing. If anyone ought to be prosecuted it ought to be Dick Armitage." Armitage declined my request for an interview.

Congressman Peter Hoekstra, who watched the affair from his seat on the House Intelligence Committee, told me he asked the CIA several times to provide information on Wilson's trip: Who ultimately approved it? Was there any confidentiality agreement that Wilson violated? The Agency never provided answers.

"I think the Wilson trip was one of the strangest assignments that I can imagine," Hoekstra said. "Not a lot of clear detail as to what was expected of him when he went. No clear idea as to who assigned him to go and no idea of whatever happened to the material that he collected when he came back. If anything it was a bad investment of the CIA's money to pay for this."

It was more than a bad investment for the CIA. It was a bad investment for America, wasting untold taxpayer dollars on the subsequent investigation and distracting the administration of the commander in chief in a time of war. And it was another wound the White House suffered compliments of the CIA.

CHAPTER 7

SOURCES AND METHODS

"The global nature of the war, the nature of the enemy, and the need for fast, efficient operations in hunting down and rooting out terrorist networks around the world have all contributed to the need for an expanded role for the special operations forces. We are transforming that command to meet that need."

Defense Secretary Donald Rumsfeld, January 7, 2003

Two months before the 2006 congressional elections, the White House figured it was a good time to put out a list of accomplishments in the half-decade since the September 11 attacks. In a few weeks, Defense Secretary Donald Rumsfeld would lose his job amid great criticism, but this White House list highlighted an area in which Rumsfeld was invaluable: providing intelligence where the CIA could not.

The twenty-one-page "Successes and Challenges" news release pointed out obvious accomplishments: al Qaeda camps eliminated from Afghanistan, Saddam removed from Iraq, Libya renouncing nuclear weapons. "Before 9/11, Pakistan and Saudi Arabia were not taking active measures to combat support to terrorists," the White House reported. "Today, they stand with the United States as key allies."

On page six, the report listed some of the most important terrorists who had been rounded up or killed, people like Abu Faraj al-Libi, al Qaeda's number-three man, and Hamza Rabi'a, al Qaeda's chief of external operations. Also on the list was one of the most vicious terrorists ever created, a man who pledged allegiance to Osama bin Laden, who gladly beheaded victims for Internet video, who sent young Arab jihadists to "martyrdom," and who conspired to kill thousands of innocent civilians. The report contained one unremarkable sentence on the death of Abu Musab al-Zarqawi. Left out was any sense of the concentrated high-tech manhunt the CIA and the military had mounted to find the worst terrorist since bin Laden.

What I will reveal in this chapter is information never before reported, but I have been careful in keeping the detail at a level that will inform the reader without betraying information that would help America's enemies.

CHAT ROOMS

The hunt for al-Zarqawi, the most wanted man in Iraq, entered uncharted territory in 2006: Internet cafés. The CIA dispatched agents into Iraqi Internet cafes, where they downloaded, within a matter of seconds, a great intelligence breakthrough—a program that allowed the CIA to read e-mails as they were being written on café computers. As members of al-Zarqawi's organization typed e-mails, agents back home read along. The Agency calls it Digital Network Intelligence. As amazing as it was, such eavesdropping often only provided clues. Terrorists often write in code: "I've got the groceries" may mean the terrorist has acquired needed guns or bomb parts.

Also targeting Internet cafés was one of the big players in the hunt for al-Zarqawi: Task Force Orange, a six-hundred-person military spy unit. The e-mails captured by the CIA and Task Force Orange could tell eavesdroppers where to focus electronic intercepts. Al Qaeda operatives in Iraq used cell phones constantly to coordinate bombings. Seized cell phones often provided a list of key phone numbers to monitor.

The CIA played a key role in the hunt for al-Zarqawi, but in many ways, the most valuable player was Defense Secretary Donald Rumsfeld.

RUMSFELD'S WAR

Rumsfeld was the man chiefly responsible for getting the Pentagon involved in developing actionable intelligence for the War on Terror. He had complained in a 2002 memo to policy guru Douglas Feith that the armed forces were not organized for manhunts, and so he set out to change that. Rumsfeld enlarged the DIA and in March 2003 made Stephen Cambone the first undersecretary of defense for intelligence. But it wasn't enough. Rumsfeld was determined to make his special operations forces integral components in America's intelligence war against the terrorists. His chief terrorist-hunting force was Joint Special Operations Command (JSOC), headquartered in a highly secure fenced compound at Fort Bragg.

There, the elite Army Delta Force and Navy SEAL Team 6 planned and practiced counter-terrorism. These daring commandos often relied on intelligence from others, and Rumsfeld wanted to move it in-house. In 2006 he assigned Task Force Orange to JSOC.

Task Force Orange, known under various names throughout its history but as Grey Fox at the outset of the War on Terror, performed amazingly daring missions. It had its own air fleet at Baltimore/Washington International Airport. Its members flew into countries under assumed names, principally to track people or intercept communications. The NSA, for all its eavesdropping technology, cannot penetrate a fiber-optic telephone line. That's why U.S. Navy submarines are used to find and splice undersea communications cables. On land, Grey Fox/Task Force Orange can do the same thing. Operators enter the targeted country, find the line they want to intercept, dig it up if need be, and attach a listening device.

Task Force Orange has another trick. In a war zone, it operates small planes equipped with listening and imaging devices. One system the military does not talk about publicly is the Medium Altitude Airborne Reconnaissance System (MAARS). MAARS is a high-resolution camera that sends live video back to a command center. Its pictures are a big improvement over the grainy black-and-white pictures sent by the unmanned Predator drone. MAARS color pictures can reveal a terrorist's facial features or a vehicle's make and model. With the Predator, commandos try to follow the light- or dark-colored car. With MAARS, can they track the black 2000 Mercedes.

Rumsfeld saw Task Force Orange and JSOC as a perfect marriage, especially as the main target was the most wanted man in the world, Osama bin Laden. The Pentagon soon formed special terrorist-hunting task forces in Afghanistan and Iraq, made up of JSOC, Task Force Orange, DIA officers, and aviation elements.

JSOC maintains its largest deployed force in history in Iraq. Headquartered at the U.S. military base in Balad, JSOC usually has about 300 high-profile terrorists on its wanted list. Its strategy for finding them is to trace the terror chiefs through their terror warriors. JSOC deploys one 120-man SEAL squadron, a Delta Force unit, 800 Rangers, and more than 100 members of Task Force Orange. The SEALs are assigned mostly to Anbar Province, the al Qaeda–infested area west of Baghdad. Delta focuses on greater Baghdad, aided by members of the British Special Air Service (SAS), on which Delta Force was modeled when Colonel Charles Beckwith created it in the late 1970s. Army Rangers, a JSOC adjunct, work northern Iraq.

JSOC's core members number only a little over 1,000, including Task Force Orange, shooters, headquarters staff at Fort Bragg, logisticians, and battle-field intelligence officers. Keeping more than 300 operators in Iraq and giving others rest time back in the States means some other theater has to suffer. That other theater is Afghanistan.

The Task Force Orange–JSOC marriage has led to the capture and killing of scores of high-level al Qaeda operatives. But still on the list in 2006 was al-Zarqawi. The Jordanian-born terrorist was wreaking havoc inside Iraq. On orders from bin Laden himself, al-Zarqawi's mission was to kill as many innocent Shi'ites as possible to provoke the bloodshed and chaos of a civil war. This would be an opening for al Qaeda to seize control of portions of Iraq and establish a base from which to attack moderate Arab states. The ultimate goal was to establish an al Qaeda–controlled caliphate in Baghdad that would claim to be the supreme ruler of all Islam. Al-Zarqawi's most successful attack came in February 2006. One of his suicidal zealots blew up himself at the Golden Dome Mosque in Samarra. It triggered tit-for-tat: Sunni-Shi'ite killings spread into 2007 and forced Bush to change his Iraq strategy four years into the war.

Task Force Orange viewed al-Zarqawi as trackable. Unlike bin Laden, he was a hands-on operator. He personally met some of the foreign jihadis who entered Iraq, he did some of the planning, and he moved around the country like a field commander, encouraging his bands of murderers. Al-Zarqawi was a terrorist of the cell phone. He didn't have his own, but borrowed others', using them as mobile command posts to director terror strikes. Cell phone signals even proved a perfect way to detonate deadly improvised explosive devices (IEDs) from afar.

Using a constant cell phone signal and GPS (global positioning system), the spy teams of Task Force Orange can determine a terrorist's exact location and track him. Ali Qaed Senyan al-Harthi, one of the planners of the 2000 terrorist attack on the USS *Cole*, was tracked in this way and killed with a Hellfire missile. By 2006, Task Force Orange had grown larger. It was divided into units that did signals intelligence, human spying, and shooters. The Pentagon added a new division in 2006: Computer Network Operations.

One thing now remained: finding a way for the CIA and NSA to share Internet café intercepts. The CIA Baghdad station had a habit of not sharing tips. But JSOC, the Agency, and the NSA eventually worked out an agreement. The Joint Interagency Coordination Group, operating out of Balad, now circulates intelligence.

With all these pieces in place, the hunt for al-Zarqawi was on.

Targeting the Internet cafés produced al Qaeda operatives, who were then followed. The process: match e-mails from an al Qaeda member with cell phones that were in the area of the café at the same time. The NSA collected the phone numbers, intercepted them, and identified the speakers. The procedure created a list of al-Zarqawi's followers, including his successor, Abu Ayyub al-Masri. Task Force Orange, using its fleet of mobile ground interceptors and aircraft, tracked these followers. It was listening when an Islamic religious advisor to al Qaeda talked of visiting al-Zarqawi. Spies and spy aircraft followed him. When he traveled to al-Zarqawi's hideout near Baquba, north of Baghdad, JSOC's hands-on commander, Lieutenant General Stanley McChrystal, had his man. The Baghdad command quickly summoned two Air National Guard pilots, and an F-16 put bombs right on target. Al-Zarqawi lay dying as U.S. personnel arrived less than an hour later. Among the eyes identifying the late Abu Musab al-Zarqawi were those of McChrystal. President Bush was so impressed that he singled out McChrystal and his organization at a White House press conference.

McChrystal, handpicked by Rumsfeld, was a new kind of JSOC commander. He spent little time at his Fort Bragg headquarters—or at any headquarters, for that matter. He was a three-star general who designed raids and then went on them alongside the enlisted men.

The hit on al-Zarqawi had been a perfect operation, from Rumsfeld's point of view: military intelligence leading to a military manhunt leading to a military air strike. "Rumsfeld wanted to go over the heads of the CIA if he had to," a military officer told me. "Now he had JSOC to do what the CIA did."

JSOC had had a dry run before nabbing al-Zarqawi. Insurgents kidnapped American Jill Carroll, a freelance journalist writing an article for the *Christian Science Monitor*. When an American is nabbed in Iraq, JSOC goes into overdrive. In this case Task Force Orange picked up the communications of men linked to the kidnappers. Delta Force and SEALs started breaking down doors, killing and capturing. One raid led to information for the next raid. They later determined Carroll was usually held at a farmhouse in Baquba. JSOC, along with SAS operatives, raided the farmhouse, capturing twenty terrorists and killing five. Carroll was not there, but Task Force Orange was getting closer—as was proved when Carroll's captors suddenly released her. She was too hot, and JSOC was too good. As one special operator told me, the kidnappers had decided: "Here, you take her. Get off our backs."

THE BOX

After the September 11, 2001, attacks, Air Force lieutenant general Michael Hayden realized his organization had to change. At that time he was leading the National Security Agency, headquartered at Fort Meade, Maryland, a forty-five-minute ride from downtown Washington.

For one, the NSA did not process intercepts fast enough. By the time a recorded conversation found its way to a translation center, was put into a report, and then was sent to policymakers, it was often too late. Hayden needed more foreign-language speakers, especially in al Qaeda's Arabic, Pakistan's Urdu, Afghanistan's Pashto, and Iran's Farsi. And he needed a way to speed up the process of analysis and distribution.

The NSA has impressive capabilities, but some of its powers are more myth than reality. It cannot, despite what some conspiracy theorists contend, constantly suck up billions of communications, sift through them for "key words," find nuggets of information, and put it all in transcripts for policymakers. Such an operation would demand hundreds of thousands of analysts and significantly more satellites and ground stations than the NSA could ever have.

The NSA, like other parts of the Defense Department establishment, must target specific people, e-mail addresses, computers, phone numbers, or at least geographic areas if it is to capture the critically important conversations.

In January 2006, Hayden, who was then John Negroponte's deputy director of national intelligence, went to the National Press Club to explain the terrorist surveillance program. The *New York Times* had recently exposed, and thus destroyed, the program on its front pages. Hayden's talk, and his taking questions from anti-NSA left-wing activists, was probably the most explicit discussion ever offered by an NSA insider about an agency that was once so secret that its initials were jokingly explained as "No Such Agency."

"Look, NSA intercepts communications," Hayden said. What a difference a few years make. After September 11, the White House implored the news media not to even use the word *intercept*, so fearful was it that bin Laden operatives perhaps somehow did not know the U.S. did that.

Hayden recalled the dark days of the Clinton era, when the NSA fell behind. He talked of "criticism that [the NSA] was going deaf, that it was ossified in its thinking, that it had not and could not keep up with the changes in modern communications."

Then he addressed the myths. "I said this isn't a driftnet, all right? I said we're not there sucking up coms and then using some of these magically alleged keyword searches—'Did he say "jihad"?' I mean, that is not—do you know how much time Americans spend on the phone in international calls alone, okay? In 2003, our citizenry was on the phone in international calls alone for 200 billion minutes, okay? I mean, beyond the ethical considerations involved here, there are some practical considerations about being a driftnet. This is targeted, this is focused. This is about al Qaeda."

At Fort Meade, after September 11, Hayden knew something else. This war on al Qaeda would be fought by small military groups who needed pinpoint intelligence, and fast. He needed to take the NSA from a national asset to a battlefield asset. As he told the press club, "After the attacks, I exercised some options I've always had that collectively better prepared us to defend the homeland."

He created a new unit, the Office of Target Reconnaissance and Survey (OTRS), at Fort Meade and gave it money to come up with new gadgets. Hayden knew that if the NSA was to really make a difference, it had to get at communications in the mountains of Afghanistan and Pakistan, in the nooks and crannies where a satellite could not penetrate. A Predator drone—an unmanned, armed reconnaissance aircraft—could soak up chatter. The CIA flew four of them in Pakistan. But drones could not, in the lingo of the spy trade, provide "persistent" coverage.

Engineers at the OTRS had an answer: it gave the mountains ears. A remote, battery-powered sensor could be placed along Afghanistan's mountain ridges and pointed at Pakistan, where the Taliban and al Qaeda retreat to regroup and try to reestablish training camps. Remote sensors already existed, but an operator had to go to them and retrieve the recorded conversations. The new models would be linked to a secure communications satellite. Captured words would be relayed to translation centers around the world, depending on the language of the intercept. Transcripts and analyses would then quickly go to joint CIA-JSOC stations abroad. There are about thirty such boxes placed on mountain ridges along the border, and the CIA has a smaller number in Pakistan that it uses to bug suspected safe houses. The boxes have their own codenames that change frequently.

The remote sensors have delivered big dividends. The sensors have let the U.S. listen in on militant groups in Pakistan's Waziristan and Bajaur, government-designated tribal regions where Osama bin Laden and his second in command, Ayman al-Zawahiri, are thought to be hiding in villages and caves. Their radio conversations may escape aerial detection, but they cannot avoid the boxes.

In October 2006, the boxes hit pay dirt. Consistent chatter came from a site near the town of Khar: the boxes had located a camp. Tribal leaders claimed it was a madrassa, a Muslim school. But the talk captured by the box did not concern math and history. Men were heard giving military orders: who would go on patrol that night, who was getting the guns and ammunition. Analysts concluded it was a school, all right: a school training young terrorists to become suicide bombers.

In October, an air strike demolished the compound, killing eighty people. Musharraf's government took credit, saying helicopter gunships had leveled the place. Perhaps. But the CIA has conducted similar strikes using multiple Predators, and Musharraf would likely have calculated that disclosing a CIA role would have made his countrymen's wrath even worse.

Four years earlier, the Defense Science Board's 2002 report had called for covert listening devices that can continuously monitor areas where the enemy operates. The NSA met that challenge in a program I'm disclosing for the first time.

WE'RE LISTENING

Michael Hayden realized that satellites were not what they used to be. Most floated around the world using technologies designed in the 1970s. They were meant to listen to military-grade communications, which send strong signals, in the Soviet Union and Communist China. But terrorists use cell phones, which weren't around in the 1970s, and short-range radios, favored by al Qaeda. Their signals are often too weak for an orbiting satellite to pick up. What's more, the Internet and al Qaeda grew up together in the 1990s.

To overcome the shortcomings of satellites, Hayden's OTRS quickly produced the remote sensors that proved so productive in Afghanistan. But the NSA needed more. It spawned what is called the Digital Network Intelligence program to snatch communication from the Internet. Digital Network Intelligence, the CIA, and Task Force Orange surf the Internet to monitor known terrorist websites and e-mail addresses, or to plant bugs, as the CIA did in the search for al-Zarqawi.

The OTRS has produced other gadgets, including mobile sensors for the Predator drone and for vehicles used by Task Force Orange. The NSA also took the lead in developing the technology that allows Task Force Orange to pinpoint cell phone locations. The Army uses a mobile sensor to augment what the NSA does, and intelligence officers operate a system called Prophet/Cobra that can intercept signals between a cell phone tower and a cell phone.

All these systems are in use in Afghanistan and Iraq. Task Force Orange flies aircraft along the border with Iran to soak up signals from cell phone towers. The data is then transferred to Fort Meade for decryption and analysis.

Iran allows senior al Qaeda members to travel from Afghanistan through Tehran to Iraq. This is another example of a Shi'ite country like Iran cooperating with the Sunni al Qaeda in a common cause: killing Americans. In 2006, the NSA picked up the voice of Abdul Hadi al-Iraqi, a Mosul native who served as bin Laden's liaison to al-Zarqawi. The U.S. tracked al-Iraqi from Quetta, in Pakistan, to Iran, but never pinpointed his location in Iraq. Based on intercepted chat room conversations, al-Iraqi at one point was viewed as the heir apparent to al-Zarqawi.

The CIA finally captured al-Iraqi, its biggest al Qaeda prize in three years, in late 2006. Officers secretly questioned him for months until they believed the closest person to being al Qaeda's number-three had coughed up all he knew. In April 2007, the CIA moved al-Iraqi to the military prison at Guantanamo Bay, Cuba. He became the fifteenth so-called high-value detainee, joining other top henchmen of al Qaeda, terrorists such as Khalid Sheikh Mohammed and a man known simply as Hambali.

While the Iranian border is a crossing point for al Qaeda leaders, the Syrian boundary is the infiltration point for Arabs, mostly from Saudi Arabia and North Africa, who answer al Qaeda's call for jihad in Iraq. They arrive in Damascus, move to safe houses near the border, and then enter Iraq. At border posts, they flash fake passports (an al Qaeda specialty). Otherwise they sneak across the 350-mile stretch of desert. Once inside Iraq, the volunteer murderers hook up with al Qaeda handlers in far-flung cells around the country. Al Qaeda set up this flow of human destructors soon after Baghdad fell in April 2003. It has continued, mostly unabated, for more than four years. About a dozen suicide jihadis enter each month. A northern smuggling route takes them through Mosul along the Tigris River to Baghdad. A central path moves north of the Euphrates River to the capital. The heavily traveled southern road takes jihadis down the Euphrates into villages in Anbar Province, where al-Zarqawi set up his shop of horrors in 2003.

Al Qaeda makes sure to keep the new arrivals separate from each other. No bomber knows what the other will do. Handlers fill their heads with anti-Western propaganda and the glory of "martyrdom" (suicidal mass murder). Their assignment comes a day before their mission. Some falter at the last minute; a few have been strapped to the steering wheel of a car or truck bomb and given sedatives. U.S. interrogators who have questioned captured jihadis often compare the Islamists to gang members: misdirected young people looking for a purpose in life. A teenager from Egypt said he had trouble meeting girls and was looking forward to Islam's promise of seventy-two virgins in martyrdom. Al Qaeda organizers themselves typically refer to Arab men coming to Iraq to kill themselves and innocent others in a suicide bombing as "sheep," which shows the terrorists' cynicism as well as their fanaticism. (Al Qaeda receives many female applicants, but few are accepted because of the objections of Muslim fundamentalists.)

To patrol the border, the Army focuses a mobile interceptor called Hammer on border areas to pick up cell phone talk that could tip off a border crossing. There are also Task Force Orange operatives in the U.S. embassy in Damascus who receive NSA transcripts (called "klieg lights") to find jihadist locations. The embassy in Damascus passes information on terrorist safe houses to the government of Syrian president Bashar al-Assad. But rarely does Syria, a U.S.-designated sponsor of terrorism, act on this information. Occasionally it will raid a safe house, apparently as a token to the U.S. or because Assad wants to make sure the jihadis realize who the boss is. Syria will allow safe haven to cooperative terrorists, but will crush terrorists who want to bring down the regime (as al Qaeda ultimately does).

U.S eavesdropping along the Syrian border sometimes picks up surprises. One night last year, Task Force Orange heard the voice of an Iraqi. "I will meet the shepherd to help him tend the sheep," the voice said. It was the kind of code that indicated more suicide bombers were on the way. The U.S. tracked the man's phone. The voice turned out to be that of a senior Iraqi border guard who was taking bribe money from al Qaeda agents to let terrorists into the country. The incident underscored what commanders already suspected— that the porous Iraqi border, made more porous by the corruption of Iraqi border guards, was funneling terrorists into the country. The United States also believes it has identified the chief organizer of these border crossings: a man named Abu Muhammed who works in Syria. But just as with the growing evidence of Iranian support for Iraqi insurgents, a great deal of intelligence is not acted upon for diplomatic or political reasons.

But communication intelligence is mounting. To intercept calls, the NSA needs phone numbers. One way it gets them is through the Tailored Access Operations system (TAO). This system penetrates the computers of main telephone switching stations and collects phone numbers and data needed to break encryptions. The phone numbers are used for link analysis. The NSA can identify a terror cell by matching numbers on Fort Meade's databases. Another way is when troops capture terrorist cell phones and simply take the numbers from a cell phone's memory. Some targets believe they can trick the NSA by changing phones. But Fort Meade's link analysis defeats them.

Aside from the NSA's number databases, the voices on the intercepts are fed to NSA stations around the world where language analysts are trained to recognize the voices of key terrorists. It is public knowledge that the intelligence community needs more foreign-language speakers. The problem is actually even worse than acknowledged. One of the reasons the United States, Great Britain, Canada, Australia, and New Zealand—the so-called "Five Eyes"— share the job of intelligence analysis is because there are only four certified Kurdish speakers in those five countries cleared for exposure to NSA's secrets and to listen to intercepts. The NSA has sent recruiters to Muslim communities in Michigan in hopes of signing up interpreters. But these missions have failed because virtually every recruit has something in his or her background to prevent top-secret clearance.

The U.S. requires telephone companies to install lines and switching stations that can by tapped by the FBI. The same requirement is in place in Iraq. The new government set up a law enforcement technical center, using American systems that allow access by the CIA and NSA.

To manage the volume of intercepts, the U.S. set up two joint interagency task forces, one in Afghanistan and one in Iraq. Its leaders—including the CIA station chiefs, an NSA code-breaker, and a JSOC representative—meet as the Joint Interagency Coordination Group to decide how to handle the intelligence that has been gathered.

THE RULES

If the American public is to fully understand why the United States has not killed bin Laden and Ayman al-Zawahiri, it has to understand the rules of engagement along the Pakistan-Afghanistan border.

America's chief hunter of high-value terrorist targets is JSOC. The most wanted are bin Laden and al-Zawahiri. They are in Pakistan. JSOC cannot go into Pakistan—unless there is a perfect alignment of diplomatic, political, intelligence, and military forces.

The rules of engagement in the border region limit the American military to a light force; the Pentagon does not want another Black Hawk Down situation in such a politically volatile area. A light force means JSOC needs precise intelligence. Knowing the village or even the street where bin Laden and al-Zawahiri might be hiding will not do—JSOC needs an address. If such intelligence came through, then—and only then—the American secretary of defense is authorized to send the special ops forces after them. The CIA and JSOC maintain joint stations along Afghanistan's border with Pakistan; while the Agency alone controls access to Pakistan, commandos can cross the border if they are in hot pursuit.

Another problem is Iraq. The four-year-old war has demanded much of JSOC's assets. There are simply more targets to chase in Iraq, where al Qaeda operates a network of several thousand. JSOC once had a robust force in Afghanistan. But as the Iraq insurgency grew, the force shrank to just 30 SEALs, augmented by about 100 Rangers. By contrast, JSOC commands 120 Delta soldiers, 120 SEALs, 800 Rangers, and a large deployment of Task Force Orange operatives in Iraq.

Bin Laden is believed to be surrounded by a small security force. Neither his voice nor al-Zawahiri's has surfaced on any intercept since they escaped the allied invasion of Afghanistan in December 2001. U.S. intelligence believes that it has, occasionally, located one of bin Laden's drivers, but it has not produced actionable intelligence.

HAMBALI

In the summer of 2003, a senior Pentagon official traveled to Thailand to help the CIA. The Agency wanted to catch Riduan Isamuddin, an Indonesian better known as Hambali. He ran Jemaah Islamiyah, a South Asia terror group linked to al Qaeda and responsible for a series of bombings, including the 2002 blast in Bali aimed at Australian tourists. In 2000 Hambali met with two of the September 11 hijackers, Khalid al-Mihdhar and Nawaf al-Hazmi.

Hambali, the only non-Arab to sit on al Qaeda's leadership council, was not as careful as his mentor, Osama bin Laden. While bin Laden kept on the move and stayed away from electronic communications, Hambali was known to communicate by phone. The CIA, which operated a base in the Thai city of Hat Yai, needed listening devices in-country to intercept Hambali's calls to his common-law wife in southern Thailand. The senior Pentagon official was able to make the arrangements with the Thai government, and the sophisticated eavesdropping equipment arrived.

In August, Hambali called his wife in Thailand, telling her he was on his way home for a visit. A joint force of Thai and American forces stormed the house, killing two of Hambali's aides and wounding the terror master. The CIA had collared one of the most wanted men in the world.

Hambali was packed aboard a Jordanian C-130 plane headed to a secret jail in Jordan for interrogation. The plane was equipped with video equipment that allowed officials in Washington to watch Hambali's onboard interrogation, in the hope of receiving actionable intelligence. It was one of the CIA's most successful renditions, done with the complete cooperation of Thai authorities, and with the important assistance of the Jordanians, whose interrogators convinced Hambali to talk (by sticking a finger in his wound).

The Hambali snatch stood as an example of an extraordinary rendition that worked. Unlike the botched operations in Europe, the Thai rendition was fully within the looser parameters of Thailand's laws. No Thai judicial body shed any tears over Hambali. Even Hambali's home country of Indonesia told the United States it could keep him. Even though they issued pro forma public denials, the Thais readily worked with U.S. military and intelligence officials. The Pentagon established a not-so-secret base in Thailand from which troops could be moved quickly for anti-terrorist operations.

President Bush acknowledged in September 2006 that the CIA had held high-value targets at CIA-run prisons. Hambali, along with other key terrorists such as September 11 mastermind Khalid Sheikh Mohammed, eventually changed their addresses to Guantanamo Bay, Cuba

LONG LIVE THE KING

Jordan's King Abdullah II came to Washington in March 2007 to receive the kind of welcome reserved for the best American allies: he was invited to give a speech to a joint session of Congress. Abdullah, trained by U.S. Green Berets as a young army officer, stood as American's strongest ally in the Middle East, both publicly and behind the scenes. Jordanian intelligence not only cooperated with American intelligence, but also housed high-value al Qaeda operatives and performed valuable cloak-and-dagger missions against terrorist targets.

In March 2007, King Abdullah talked about the importance of Palestinian-Israeli peace. "No Palestinian father should be helpless to feed his family and build a future for his sons and daughters," the king said. "No Israeli mother should fear when her child boards a bus. Not one more generation should grow up thinking that violence and conflict are the norm."

Abdullah avoided a direct reference to his prime enemy, al Qaeda, which has long wanted to destabilize Jordan and turn its Sunni Palestinian population into Osama bin Laden disciples. But Abdullah knew al Qaeda had come within a few hours of bringing down his regime.

In 2005, Jordan's prominent role as America's chief Middle East ally in the War on Terror was underscored by a foiled attack. The press reported that authorities penetrated a plot to use chemicals and explosives to inflict mass casualties in the capital of Amman. What the press did not report is that police not only stopped what would have been one of the world's worst terror attacks, but it also saved the regime of King Abdullah II.

Authorities arrested Azmi Jayyousi, the cell's ringleader, and seized tons of explosives and chemicals. Jordanian state-run television showed Jayyousi confessing. He took his orders from Abu Musab al-Zarqawi, the Jordanian who went to Iraq to start a spree of killings there as the head of al Qaeda's operations in Iraq.

"I took explosives courses, poisons high level, then I pledged allegiance to Abu Musab al-Zarqawi, to obey him without any questioning," the captive said. He had traveled to Iraq for training and then returned to Jordan to plot the destruction of key government buildings.

The al Qaeda plot had involved creating a binary chemical weapon (one that combines two chemicals to cause an explosion) including a blistering agent. Two trucks, crammed with chemicals and explosives, were to be driven by suicide bombers at high speeds and crashed into each other, creating an enormous blast and a chemical cloud that could have killed thousands.

But Jordanian intelligence penetrated the operation before it could be launched. Authorities took about a pound of the chemicals the terrorists intended to use out into the desert to test their potency in a controlled explosion. The soldiers involved in the exercise, explosives experts, retreated to what they thought was a safe distance. But the remotely controlled explosion covered an enormous distance—more than sixteen miles—and burned some of the participants.

According to high-level Jordanian sources, had al-Zarqawi succeeded in his terrorist attack in Amman that spring, as many as 80,000 people would have died. King Abdullah would almost certainly have been overthrown for failing to stop it. The king's men would have been endangered by a possible Palestinian revolt (about half of Jordan's population is Palestinian), urged on by Iran and Syria, or perhaps a military coup.

What the Jordanians stopped was an attack using weapons of mass destruction, planned by terrorists linked to al Qaeda. According to high Jordanian sources, the chemicals, explosives, and trucks entered Jordan from Syria.

The incident highlighted the high quality of Jordan's intelligence service as well as the extreme danger of al Qaeda acquiring biological, chemical, or nuclear weapons.

PLAYING THE HORN

Special operations forces have also turned the tide of battle in two other areas targeted by al Qaeda: the Philippines and the Horn of Africa.

Donald Rumsfeld realized the Horn's importance from the beginning of the War on Terror. Once bin Laden was ousted from Afghanistan, he would be looking for a new headquarters in an essentially ungoverned Islamic country. Somalia fit the bill. The defense secretary quickly established a task force in Djibouti, bordering Somalia. From there, Special Forces have deployed to neighboring countries to train friendly government troops in counter-insurgency tactics.

The Combined Joint Task Force–Horn of Africa worked particularly closely with the Ethiopian army. When the Ethiopians invaded Somalia in early 2006 to oust an al Qaeda–linked regime, they relied on U.S. training, and, one source told me, U.S. advice on the war plan.

Across the Red Sea in Yemen, Special Forces revamped the Yemeni army, which proceeded to eradicate the al Qaeda network that had bombed the USS *Cole* in 2000.

In the Philippines in 2001, the al Qaeda–linked terrorist group Abu Sayyaf controlled its own island, Basilan. Its particularly vicious terrorists used it as a base for launching terror attacks and kidnappings. Rumsfeld dispatched a large number of conventional units and Special Forces to train the Philippine army in tactics and intelligence. With that training the Filipinos recovered the island of Basilan and killed many Abu Sayyaf leaders.

In fact, in every military theater around the world, the United States, working with moderate governments, has badly damaged al Qaeda. The one big exception is Iraq, which al Qaeda has made its chief war front. There the United States is bogged down fighting an insurgency driven in part by al Qaeda, in part by elements loyal to the former Ba'ath regime of Saddam Hussein, and in part by the most important national supporter of Islamic terrorism: the militant regime in Iran.

CHAPTER 8

TARGET: IRAN

"Across the board, the intelligence community knows disturbingly little about the nuclear programs of many of the world's most dangerous actors."

Robb Silberman Commission on the Intelligence Capabilities of the United States Regarding Weapons of Mass Destruction, March 31, 2005

Two months after al Qaeda's attack on America, Michael Ledeen headed for an important meeting at the White House. In those intense, post-attack days the Bush people hungered for any information they could get on rogue states and terrorism. Ledeen said he had some. The American Enterprise Institute scholar was a fixture in conservative national security circles. He had come to prominence in the 1980s as an advisor to Secretary of State Alexander Haig. Few at the State Department were as fervently anti-Soviet as Ledeen. When he thought State wasn't tough enough in condemning Soviet pressure on Poland, Ledeen threatened to resign, proclaiming, "I'm here to bring down the Soviet empire."

In the think tank world, Ledeen turned out books and articles on the evils of terror regimes such as Iraq and Iran. He pestered the CIA for its incompetence and the Clinton administration for its timidity. "I don't think Moses could fix the CIA," he griped. Ledeen's anti-terror fervor runs in the family: his son is a Marine office who fought in Iraq, patrolling dangerous Anbar Province and al Qaeda hotbeds like Haditha.

Ledeen also maintained a link to a man deemed a pariah by the CIA and the Washington establishment. Manucher Ghorbanifar, an Iranian exile living in Paris, was part of the rogue's gallery of participants in the Iran-Contra scandal of the late 1980s. An international arms dealer, Ghorbanifar had helped arrange Israel's delivery of 508 anti-tank missiles to Iran. The CIA then labeled him an unsavory character, a liar, and a cheat. Langley considered him persona non grata and executed a "burn notice" ending his relationship as a source.

But Ledeen, committed to overthrowing the terror-sponsoring regime in Iran, considered Ghorbanifar a good source on what was happening inside the treacherous halls of government in Tehran. "Sometimes he's right. Sometimes, like everyone else, he's wrong," Ledeen said. "I don't know of any other man who has better insights into what is going on inside Iran."

After the September 11, 2001, attacks, Ghorbanifar told Ledeen about two Iranians, close to the ruling mullahs, who were willing to talk. It was the sort of off-the-books contact that Reaganites had thrived on—and sometimes suffered through—in the heady Cold War days of two decades before. Excited, Ledeen traveled the short distance from his downtown office to the lair of Stephen Hadley, then President Bush's deputy national security advisor. There too was NSC aide Zalmay Khalilzad, who would go on to serve as ambassador to Afghanistan and Iraq, and then to the United Nations. Ledeen proposed a mission to Rome, where Ghorbanifar would match them up with the two Iranians, one of whom, purportedly, was especially well informed.

At the White House that day, Ledeen declared, "I know you are going to throw me out." But Hadley, eager for any information on terror-sponsoring states, sounded enthusiastic. Days later, Ledeen learned the mission was on. The White House tasked the Pentagon, which offered up two policy shop workers: Iranian expert Harold Rhode and Larry Franklin, a Defense Intelligence Agency analyst. The Italian government agreed to provide a setting for the debriefings. Washington's envoy to Rome was on board.

All flew to Rome, Ledeen at his own expense. Over several days, the Iranian sources talked. Ghorbanifar sat in the background, occasionally helping with Farsi-English translations. Ledeen said, "In this case, we knew these sources were reliable. We knew the one had possibly accurate information on Iranian terrorism." Among the tidbits: Iran had organized hunter-killer teams to attack Americans in Afghanistan. The key Iranian source identified who organized them and who led them.

Franklin made a point of briefing Colonel John F. Mulholland, who led special operations forces in Afghanistan. "Everybody was happy," Ledeen recalled of the apparent intelligence coup. Well, not everybody.

When Franklin's reporting reached the CIA, director George Tenet hit the roof. He complained to the White House that Ledeen's team had circumvented the Agency. Secretary of State Colin Powell also complained, stating that Ghorbanifar was off-limits. To the CIA, the Rome mission seemed another attempt by the Pentagon to supplant the Agency as the nation's intelligence service. The CIA felt threatened and counter-attacked. The administration cut off ties with Ghorbanifar, and Franklin, an Air Force Reserve colonel, ended up as the target of an FBI probe. He was sentenced to a dozen years in prison for passing information about the Iranian threat to pro-Israeli lobbyists in an attempt to get the word, which he could not do from his position at the Defense Department, to the National Security Council.

Ledeen said the CIA never attempted to talk to the two Iranian informants. Under the pressures of war, and with few or no sources inside al Qaeda, the Agency was supposed to end its policy of eschewing unsavory sources. But Ghorbanifar did not qualify. And those who did talk to him faced the Agency's ire. "I consider this case one of the most incredible things I ever saw," Ledeen said.

In interviews with current and former CIA officers, I received the same message. If the CIA is in fact working any agents in Iran, they must not be very good. The Agency knows very little about the inner workings of the world of the radical mullahs striving for nuclear weapons and Israel's destruction. "The CIA has always been terrible about Iran," Ledeen said. History backs him up. The Agency's Tehran station was surprised by the 1979 revolution that replaced the shah with the world's first hard-line Islamic regime. It was slow to detect Iran's growing incursions into Iraq. Its predictions on when Tehran will have the bomb are fuzzy.

Several years later, Ledeen got a call from Langley. Stephen Kappes, then the director of the clandestine service, wanted to have lunch. Ledeen, a vocal critic of the Agency, had advocated covert action to bring down the Iranian mullahs. "We probably have sixty million people in Iran who want to bring down this regime," he said. "If you can't bring down a regime with sixty million people, give up."

The two met at a McLean, Virginia, restaurant a few miles from CIA headquarters. Ledeen made his case for intervention. Kappes made his case against it. "He said, 'Iran is coming along just fine,'" Ledeen said. He quoted Kappes as saying, "Give it another ten years or so. If you get us involved, who knows what will happen?"

But the real question was whether the CIA had any idea of what would happen, U.S. intervention or not. The Robb-Silberman commission studied the intelligence community's knowledge about Iran's nuke program, but declined to declassify any of its findings. Congressman Pete Hoekstra, however, was not as timid. He ordered an unclassified staff report that bluntly chastised the CIA for not knowing more about Iran.

"There is a great deal about Iran that we do not know," the August 2006 report said. "The United States lacks critical information needed for analysis to make many of their judgments with confidence about Iran and there are many significant information gaps. A special concern is major gaps in our knowledge of Iranian nuclear, biological and chemical programs."

The report stopped just short of saying that the CIA has few—if any—agents in Iran: "The intelligence community lacks the ability to acquire essential information necessary to make judgments on these essential topics."

It goes back to what a veteran CIA covert intelligence agent told me. If the CIA had wanted sources inside Iran, it should have recruited them decades ago; reliable human intelligence is a matter of long-term relationships with sources.

FREE THE MEK

Ledeen was not the only outsider trying get the administration to talk to Iranian outcasts. In the spring of 2006, as Iran's deadly hand in Iraq's affairs came to the forefront, retired Air Force lieutenant general Thomas McInerney traveled to Paris with a group of other like-minded conservatives. McInerney, a Vietnam War fighter pilot, wanted Bush to order air strikes on Iran's thirty or so nuclear sites.

A nuclear-armed Iran, with its long-range ballistic missiles and fanatical leaders, could lead to a Middle East Armageddon. If the Iranian regime of Mahmoud Ahmadinejad was true to his word and tried to eliminate Israel, it would mean nuclear war. Classified DIA documents I obtained showed that Israel maintained an arsenal of eighty-two nuclear warheads.

McInerney ran a group known as the Iran Policy Committee, which publicized Iran's misdeeds, such as a shipment of highly explosive roadside bombs into Iraq to kill Americans. McInerney was more than just the chairman of a fairly obscure group. He had also become part of Donald Rumsfeld's kitchen cabinet. Rumsfeld viewed McInerney as a tough ex-warrior on whom he relied for advice. When Rumsfeld resigned in November 2006, McInerney was one of the few retired officers he invited in for a farewell lunch at the Pentagon.

Waiting for McInerney in Paris was the charismatic leader of the National Council of Resistance of Iran. Maryam Rajavi, an Iranian exile, oversaw a varied collection of expatriates determined to oust the mullahs from Tehran. Among them was the notorious militia Mujahedin-e Khalq, or MEK. The MEK played rough, executing a number of bombings that killed high-ranking members of Iran's revolutionary government. Saddam Hussein provided the militia with camps near the Iranian border that were close enough to pester his arch-rivals.

McInerney believed Rajavi's National Council, unlike the CIA, had good contacts in Iran. After all, the National Council had released evidence in 2002 that Iran operated a secret uranium enrichment facility at Natanz. Alerted, the United Nation's International Atomic Energy Agency (IAEA) demanded an inspection and confirmed the council's information.

"The CIA isn't even in their league. These dissidents are actual doers," McInerney said of Rajavi's followers. "You find most Iranian dissidents sitting in L.A. drinking cappuccinos."

McInerney's entourage sat for hours that day in Paris, listening to Rajavi's vision of a democratic Iran. Pursuant to Muslim custom, she wore a head scarf and did not shake hands with the men. "All I want is someone to destabilize that regime," she said through an interpreter. McInerney, the hardened fighter pilot, was mesmerized. "It was a brilliant dissertation," he said. She spoke without notes for hours on the history of Iran and what it could become without the backward-thinking mullahs. McInerney cites that meeting as the basis for his attempts to convince Washington to bomb Iran and undermine the regime.

There was a hitch in the prospect of Washington forging ties with Rajavi. In 1997, the Clinton administration shifted policy and tried to reach out to Iran's leaders, then seen as more "moderate" than previous ones. It met one of Tehran's demands by putting the MEK on the State Department's official list of terror groups, right alongside Lebanon's Hezbollah and the Central Asian Islamic Jihad Group. A group friendly to the United States—and which wanted American help—was suddenly as bad as al Qaeda in Washington's eyes. The Bush administration allowed the MEK to remain on the list, making it virtually impossible for the CIA to use the group's sources even if it wanted to.

But I learned that the MEK is helping American troops via unofficial back channels. When the United States invaded Iraq in 2003, American troops corralled some four thousand MEK fighters and put them under protective custody at Camp Ashra, near the border with Iran. The FBI interviewed most of them, looking for criminals. After they were cleared, the U.S. military let the MEK maintain contacts with their sources inside Iran. In this way the MEK has provided vital information about Iranian treachery. MEK sources were able to pinpoint the building in Ibril in Iraq where members of the Qods Force, the deadly special operations arm of Iran's Revolutionary Guard Corps, were posing as diplomats under fake identities. The MEK has helped the U.S. military deconstruct and analyze the explosively formed projectiles (EFPs) made in Iran with the sole purpose of penetrating armor and killing U.S. troops.

The CIA will not utilize the MEK, but the military will—because American lives are on the line and the MEK's intelligence can help. McInerney's committee held a press conference in January 2007 to show off the latest intelligence findings from Rajavi's group. The MEK believes Iran produces its EFPs in the Lavizan neighborhood of northern Tehran. Charged with making the explosives is the Qods Force, who take orders directly from Tehran's interior ministry, which reports to the ruling mullahs.

When he returned to Washington, McInerney went to the Pentagon to brief senior policymakers. Then he crossed the Potomac for an audience with White House National Security Council people. His message: the MEK should be an asset, not a pariah. Take it off the State Department list of terror groups. All his efforts were to no avail; an administration official told me, "They are terrorists. There will be no change."

In 2007, McInerney traveled to Tampa for a conference on intelligence collection and the war. As he has done in other forums, the hawkish ex-general ("Tom wants to bomb everything," a retired three-star general said of him) laid out what he believes is a relatively simply plan for bombing Iran.

More than a dozen B-2 stealth fighters would be positioned in the region and would crisscross the country, using penetrating bombs to destroy Iran's underground nuke sites. Around 150 F-16s would capture Iran's airspace and hit military installations, aided by 36 F-117 stealth fighters targeting air defense missiles and radars. In all, 25,000 "aim points" would be attempted. "We could do it in one or two days," he told me.

McInerney has many detractors who believe a bombing campaign would only further inflame Shi'ites in Iraq, prompt Iran to sabotage governments in the region, and spur Iranians who might otherwise be pro-American to side with the mullahs.

One such critic is Douglas Macgregor, the bane of the Army's staid general officer corps. A strong-willed retired colonel, the iconoclastic Macgregor has authored three books on reforming the Army. Most generals view his ideas as radical, but Donald Rumsfeld took a liking to Macgregor in his early days as defense secretary and adopted his ideas of reorganizing Army units into modular combat brigade teams. In a conversation one day with retired Army major general Robert Scales, a former Army War College commandant who cares deeply about his service, I asked about Macgregor. There was silence, then, "Next topic."

"We don't have to bomb Iran," Macgregor told me. "There are lots of reasons to try diplomacy, if we are patient. We can build a relationship with Iran that will allow us to work as friends, not enemies. Shia Islam is not the same as Sunni Islam. They tend to hate the same people we do."

Added Macgregor, who now lectures and advises corporations, "Iran is an interesting marriage of theocracy and democracy, and theocracy is losing. If we stay out of it and find a way to expand relations the way we did through the Eastern Bloc, I think ultimately we will become friends, not enemies. I think the mullahs will eventually drop off. One thing the mullahs have failed miserably at is the economy."

Mike McConnell, John Negroponte's successor as the director of national intelligence, went before Congress in the winter of 2007 to deliver to lawmakers the intelligence community's annual assessment of threats facing America. Senator Carl Levin, the chairman of the Armed Services Committee, was particularly interested in when Iran might be able to build its first nuclear bomb. The date is important. Most war scenarios rest on this logic: You bomb Iran before, not after, it owns a nuclear arsenal. Don't give the world another North Korea, a rogue despot with nukes.

"Iran and North Korea are of particular concern, and these regimes have pursued nuclear programs in defiance of United Nations Security Council restrictions," McConnell said. "We assess that Tehran seeks to develop nuclear weapons and has shown greater interest in drawing out the negotiations rather than reaching an acceptable diplomatic solution. This is a very dangerous situation, as nuclear Iran could prompt destabilizing countermoves by other states in this volatile region. While our information is incomplete, we estimate Iran could produce a nuclear weapon by early to mid next decade." In a subsequent speech in April 2007, McConnell talked openly about having to adhere to Bush Time: rising at 4 a.m. to receive top-secret briefings so he can personally brief the president.

"My day gets to start real early and so far I'm discovering the things that I wanted to focus on occupy until somewhere around ten or eleven at night," McConnell said. "So, my biggest challenge early is just stamina. Can I stay with this? It was a little easier when I was a little younger, but that's what I'm adjusting to."

The candid remark reminded some of Goss's complaint of being exhausted months before he resigned.

The Bush administration, I can report, has abandoned plans, at least temporarily, to bomb Iran's nuclear sites as well as air defense missile batteries and facilities for the Revolutionary Guard Corps, which keep the mullahs in power.

Among officials I talked to, I sensed no urgency about contingency war planning against Iran. This is in stark contrast to 2002, when the administration felt an urgent need to act against Iraq. General Tommy Franks had presented his first formal plan (based on secret meetings he had had with Rumsfeld) to invade Iraq in April 2002.

With regard to Iran, the administration has bolstered U.S. naval forces in the region to put pressure on the mullahs, and U.S. Central Command is updating its target list, but not particularly quickly. The Air Force has a group of about twenty officers, dubbed "Checkmate," who work in a Pentagon basement office making contingency bombing plans for Iran, but few expect them to be acted upon.

The Bush administration has settled on another track. "We are following a diplomatic course, period," a senior policymaker told me. It is not just that the CIA has limited information on Iran's nuclear weapons program. The wars in Iraq and Afghanistan, the continuing low-intensity war against terror around the world, and the military's other global responsibilities are wars enough for the U.S. military. The Joint Chiefs of Staff worry that a bombing strike on Iran will lead to Iranian counter-attacks in Iraq, further destabilizing an already chaotic country and requiring American reinforcements that are unlikely to be forthcoming from an administration under political pressure from congressional Democrats to withdraw from Iraq. General Peter Pace, the Joint Chiefs chairman, privately commented in the Pentagon that the United States does not own sufficient stocks of precision weapons to do the job in Iran and still keep its military commitments in Iraq, Afghanistan, and the Pacific.

That's why Bush turned in 2007 to Navy admiral William Fallon to run Central Command, a post always previously commanded by either a Marine or a soldier. Fallon had proved his worth as a warrior-diplomat in his stint as Pacific commander. He was good at reassuring Asian allies on U.S. intentions to protect them while talking frankly with Communist China and North Korea. Fallon's job in the Persian Gulf: keep moderate Arab states in line as Bush ratchets up the pressure on Iran through a show of military force and economic sanctions.

BOLTON'S VIEW

The likelihood of a U.S. strike on Iran diminished in 2007, partly because Europe, China, and Russia finally signed on to step-by-step economic sanctions meant to put pressure on Iran's already shaky economy. Even hard-liners such as former UN ambassador John Bolton do not put the military option in the top tier of choices, even though Bolton thinks the United States will have to go beyond sanctions to prevent a nuclear-armed Iran.

"I don't think the sanctions that were adopted by the Security Council are going to work to dissuade Iran from pursuing nuclear weapons," Bolton told me. "I think it has to be much, much stronger than that. I think ultimately the only way to stop it is through regime change. I don't think the policy that they've been pursuing will be enough to stop them."

Regime change is a laudable goal. But, I asked, how do we accomplish that?

"I think mostly by capitalizing on the dissatisfaction that's so evident within Iran because of the opposition to the religious nature of the regime, the desire for a better life, the mishandling of the economy, the ethnic tensions," he responded. "I think there are a lot of factors that could go into regime change. I'm not saying it would be easy. I'm not saying it would happen quickly. But I think the possibility is very much there. I think we should be providing support above and below ground to pro-democratic forces. "

Are we doing that today?

"Certainly above ground. And I think that's the right thing to do. I don't think there is anything wrong with that. I think that's consistent with the way we operated during the Cold War. And I think to do something to stop this regime's twenty-year-long pursuit of nuclear weapons, it's well worth the effort."

How about below ground?

"I think we ought to be doing that now. I don't know myself, but I've been out of the game for a long time. When I was in New York [as UN ambassador], I wouldn't have known about it anyway."

Does America have the evidence to present to the UN that Tehran is, in fact, building the bomb?

"Sure, and I think we've done that in a variety of places, at the IAEA [International Atomic Energy Agency] and the Security Council and speeches. The full scope of Iran's program is not explainable unless they're trying to acquire nuclear weapons."

If we are at the brink, and Iran is close to assembling its first bomb, could we lay out a convincing case, beyond a reasonable doubt? We were wrong about Iraq's weapons of mass destruction programs, and some in Congress have complained that we know little about Iran's inner workings.

"I think we could lay a lot of it out. I'm not sure we would be able to lay it all out because there is a lot we don't know. That doesn't make me more sanguine about Iran's nuclear program. It worries me because it means there's much we don't know. Given what we do, I think the direction of the program is unmistakable. I wouldn't go to the UN for permission to conduct a strike anyway. But I do think if it ever came to military action, we would obviously have to be prepared to explain why we were doing it somewhere and I think we could make a very strong case why we were. My own view is the military option is not the preferable option. But if the choice is between an Iran with nuclear weapons and our use of military force, then I think the choice is clear."

So the intelligence on Iran is better than the 2002 intelligence estimate on Iraq?

"Yes, it is. What we knew about Iraq's program was really quite limited—that Saddam was keeping his nuclear scientists and technicians together. He called them the nuclear mujahadeen against the day when UN sanctions and weapons inspectors were gone when he could recreate the program." But Iraq's WMD program amounted to scientists rather than arsenals: "the intellectual capital in their heads, not tubes and materials and what not."

"What we know about Iran is more extensive than that. But also much of it is public. That's one of the things that is different. If you look at the range of IAEA reports over the past four years it's really remarkable how much evidence is out there in public and then if you add to that the examples of Iranian deceptions, refusal to cooperate with the IAEA, obstruction of the IAEA work, all of it supports the conclusion that they're seeking nuclear weapons."

Did he ever discuss with Israel its options for a military strike? (Israel has never been in a better military position to bomb Iran's network of thirty or so nuclear sites. In the 1990s and now, it has purchased long-range F-15 and F-16 aircraft and U.S. bunker-busting bombs. A few of them on the same aim point could penetrate Iran's underground enrichment sites hundreds of feet below the surface.)

"We never talked about that as such, but you know from what they're saying in Israel they consider Iran to be an existential threat to the state of Israel. It's a small country. Two or three nuclear weapons would devastate it. So it wouldn't surprise me if they were preparing for it. It would surprise me if they weren't preparing for it.

"I think when you look at a country with a nuclear weapons capability run by people like Mahmoud Ahmadinejad, who talks about wiping the state of Israel off the map, that that's a pretty glaring combination of capabilities and intentions. And if I were an Israeli I would certainly worry about it."

At what point do we attack? When Iran is making the bomb or when it has one?

"I don't think we have a lot of time before we are going to have to confront that option, because every day that goes by allows them to overcome more of the difficulties they have and get closer to a completely indigenous capability over the nuclear fuel cycle. That's what the Israelis call the 'point of no return.' That is to say, the point at which they have mastered everything they need to know and it's just a question of completing all the steps. That's not the same as having the bomb, but it's an important step."

Iran is building the Shahab family of ballistic missiles. Does Tehran plan on building one that can reach the United States?

"I think that is clearly their objective. If you're doing a ballistic missile program, what you need to do to perfect the missile that you can land on target 3,000 miles away is not that different than what you need to do to have a missile that can land on target 12,000 miles away or 15,000 miles away. So once you're in it, it's simply a question of continuing your scientific research, testing out your missile design, telemetry guidance, all of the components of the missile system, until you can get it right. I don't have any doubt that they want an ICBM capacity that really could reach across continents."

If Bolton is right, Iran's ultimate target might not be Israel, but the United States. If this is true, Langley's willful ignorance about this regime could sabotage a lot more than an administration.

BROKEN BEYOND REPAIR?

In Washington's highbrow Georgetown neighborhood, the spies came in, not from the cold, but from a pristine May evening in 2007. CIA officers current and former crowded into the second floor of Healy Hall at Georgetown University to celebrate the publication of their boss's memoir, *At the Center of the Storm*.

George Tenet had led the Agency longer than every man but one. As deputy director and then as chief spy, he had presided over some successes but also over a series of historic failures not much worth celebrating.

As al Qaeda grew bigger and deadlier, the CIA became smaller and meeker, crippled by President Clinton's budget cuts. Tenet himself admits that his beloved agency was in Chapter 11 bankruptcy.

Then came the age of terror, and with it colossal CIA mistakes. After the attacks of September 11, bipartisan panels documented those mistakes in unprecedented public reports. Critical information not shared; documents not examined; a presidential draft speech not read; few, if any, agents in

Baghdad or Tehran; an inaccurate assessment of Saddam Hussein's weapons... the list seemed endless.

Tenet had told a joint congressional inquiry that he did not view the September 11 attacks, the worst on American soil, as an intelligence failure. The statement so astounded critics that they concluded the CIA was an institution in denial.

It still is today. Tenet's book, which brought him instant wealth and the number-one berth on the *New York Times* bestseller list, shifts blame on key issues to hard-liners inside the White House and the Pentagon. Afghanistan, Tenet writes, was a crowning CIA success. Ask Pentagon planners about the CIA's performance during the fall of 2001, however, and you will get a different story.

Tenet claims the CIA alone recognized Islamic terror as a grave threat to America in the late 1990s. But if that is true, why did he allow his agency to deteriorate under the president who appointed him and who slashed his budget? Republicans say Tenet complained in closed hearings about the Clinton budget cuts. But he never took his criticisms public, he did not resign in protest, and when he asked Clinton for a $2 billion annual budget increase, he received only a pittance.

But at his book party ten years later, the atmosphere was cheery. Wine and canapés floated on trays amid the crowd of intelligence heavyweights. Tenet's publisher gushed over the first week's book sales and the gigantic first printing of 300,000 copies. In his own remarks, Tenet alluded faintly to the CIA's mistakes when he talked about the difficulty of putting together the pieces of a puzzle.

I struck up a conversation with Robert D. Walpole, a dedicated CIA employee. Walpole is now a deputy director at the Office of the Director of National Intelligence. In 2002 he played a major role in writing the Iraq National Intelligence Estimate. He defended it to me that night. First, he said, the National Intelligence Council had only a matter of weeks to produce it, as demanded by Senate Democrats. Second, the aluminum tubes issue—whether aluminum tubes acquired by Saddam Hussein had been for conventional or nuclear weapons—had been distorted in the press. Two dissenting agencies, the State Department and the Department of Energy, had both said that while the tubes were likely for conventional weapons, they *could* be used for nuclear weapons development. They did not rule it out. The CIA had been more conclusive: they were definitely for nuclear weapons. The NIE, in Walpole's view, had been an honest mistake.

Separately, I talked with Porter Goss. He declined to discuss his tenure as CIA director, saying that his actions inside the Agency should remain confidential. But he was willing to talk about his time leading the House Intelligence Committee in the 1990s.

"It was perfectly clear and true that our intelligence community had been stripped naked," Goss said. "We did not have the resources we needed."

He lauded then House Speaker Newt Gingrich for recognizing the CIA's downhill course and trying to change direction with budget increases the Clinton administration did not want.

"It was a significant turnaround," Goss said. Still, he added, "The Clinton administration was not energetically supportive of the intelligence community from my perspective as the chairman of the House Select Committee on Intelligence. I never got the impression they were worried about us losing capacity and clearly we were. We weren't just threadbare. We were threadless near the end of the 1990s."

As a nation, we are still paying for the "threadless" 1990s.

I began this book with a letter from Congressman Pete Hoekstra to President Bush. Hoekstra is a Republican partisan, for sure. But he is also a patriot who realizes more than most that radical Islam poses the greatest threat to the United States since Hitler and Stalin. In his letter, Hoekstra not only warned the president about CIA saboteurs, but also chastised the administration for keeping his committee in the dark.

Another Hoekstra letter, this one to national security advisor Stephen Hadley, closes chapter four. Congressman Hoekstra is a hands-on legislator. He knows that the center of gravity in the war against al Qaeda is the Middle East, with East Africa and North Africa as vital secondary fronts. Five years after September 11, 2001, he visited the CIA stations in the region.

He was appalled. It was almost like al Qaeda had not declared war on America. The CIA staffers were young and inexperienced, and very few of them stuck around long enough to get to know the country.

President Bush has thrown more resources at the CIA. Michael Hayden, Goss's successor, told C-SPAN that the Agency is being virtually rebuilt from the ground up. Before September 11, the Clintonites and most members of Congress failed to recognize that intelligence collection became more, not less, crucial in the post-Soviet world.

The great question now is whether the Agency can be repaired. It's an open question. But if General Hayden and his successors do succeed in remaking the CIA as the world's premier intelligence agency—as it needs to be—it can only be hoped that this lesson has been learned: the world will always be a dangerous place and America cannot afford an intelligence agency more devoted to bureaucratic turf battles than to defending the homeland.

CAST OF CHARACTERS

RICHARD ARMITAGE. Deputy secretary of state who told columnist Robert Novak, in an offhand remark, that CIA operative Valerie Plame had arranged for her husband Joseph Wilson's CIA fact-finding trip to Niger. For three years, Armitage did not disclose his role as Novak's source, while the White House underwent an arduous criminal investigation.

FULTON ARMSTRONG. CIA analyst who wrongly accused John Bolton of not clearing a speech on Cuba. Deemed pro-Castro by Bolton, Armstrong won a plum post in Europe.

JOHN BOLTON. Former undersecretary of state for arms control. CIA officer Fulton Armstrong wrongfully accused Bolton of not properly clearing a speech on Cuba and helped scuttle Bolton's nomination as United

Nations ambassador. Bush sent him to the UN on a recess appointment that expired after a year.

PRESIDENT GEORGE W. BUSH. Forty-third president of the United States. Complained about CIA leaks in private but tried to make peace with bureaucracy and rebuild the clandestine service.

AHMED CHALABI. Iraqi national who became the most celebrated opponent of Saddam Hussein in the United States. He was embraced by the White House and the Pentagon, but found himself under constant attack from the CIA.

VICE PRESIDENT DICK CHENEY. Asked the CIA to investigate an intelligence report that Iraq was seeking yellowcake in Niger. Though this was the impetus for Joseph Wilson's CIA-sponsored fact-finding trip, Cheney had neither asked for the trip nor knew of Wilson's mission.

BILL CHRISTISON. Former CIA analyst who spun conspiracy theories about the September 11 attacks.

BILL CLINTON. Forty-second president of the United States. He slashed the CIA's clandestine service, leaving America's premier intelligence agency crippled as radical Islam spread throughout the world.

SENATOR CHRISTOPHER DODD. The senior senator from Connecticut, Dodd opposed President Bush's foreign policy in Latin America.

DOUGLAS FEITH. Pentagon policy chief who wanted to discover any links among terror groups and between al Qaeda and Saddam Hussein.

PATRICK FITZGERALD. Special prosecutor leading the investigation to discover who leaked Valerie Plame's identity as a CIA operative. He subpoenaed reporters and put one in jail, but never indicted anyone for leaking Plame's identity.

FRED FLEITZ. Undersecretary of state John Bolton's chief of staff.

PORTER GOSS. A former spy in Latin America, he won election to the House of Representatives from Florida and led the House Intelligence Committee. Bush tapped him to head the CIA to reform the clandestine service and plug leaks. Goss seemed a perfect fit, but he left the Agency after less than two years, bloodied by press leaks and battles with John Negroponte.

MICHAEL HAYDEN. Air Force general who served as director of the National Security Agency and succeeded Goss at the helm of the CIA.

SEYMOUR HERSH. *New Yorker* writer who helped popularize the idea of a neoconservative conspiracy at the Pentagon.

CONGRESSMAN PETE HOEKSTRA. Succeeded Porter Goss as House Intelligence Committee chairman. Warned President Bush that the CIA had a political agenda and was out to embarrass the administration.

STEPHEN KAPPES. Veteran CIA operative who was in exile during the tenure of Porter Goss. Returned to the Agency as deputy director under General Hayden.

KAREN KWIATKOWSKI. Former Air Force officer who spun conspiracy theories from her desk in the Pentagon.

MICHAEL LEDEEN. American Enterprise Institute scholar who tried to get the CIA to work against Iranian regime.

SENATOR CARL LEVIN. Democrat from Michigan who used his position on the Senate Intelligence Committee to attack the Bush administration.

I. LEWIS "SCOOTER" LIBBY. A top aide to Vice President Dick Cheney, he was convicted of lying to the grand jury in the Plame investigation.

WILLIAM LUTI. Former Navy captain and hard-charging policymaker in the Pentagon and at the White House. As a Feith aide, he felt the sting of CIA allegations that the Bush administration was politicizing intelligence.

MICHAEL MALOOF. A longtime Pentagon analyst who studied intelligence reports on the links among terror groups. He found himself a target of the intelligence community, which moved to strip his security clearance for stepping on the CIA's turf.

MARY McCARTHY. A contributor to John Kerry's campaign, she was forced to retire from the CIA after an internal probe revealed that she had leaked to the news media.

MIKE McCONNELL. Succeeded John Negroponte as director of national intelligence.

RAY McGOVERN. Former CIA analyst who spun conspiracy theories about the September 11 attacks.

LIEUTENANT GENERAL THOMAS McINERNEY. Retired Air Force officer and co-author of *Endgame: The Blueprint for Victory in the War on Terror.*

Lobbied the administration to support dissident Iranians and advocated bombing of suspected nuclear sites in Iran.

JOHN NEGROPONTE. First director of national intelligence, the new top dog of the intelligence community—a position formerly held by the CIA director. Negroponte tried to micromanage the CIA and worked to get Goss fired.

ROBERT NOVAK. Veteran high-profile newspaper columnist famous for his scoops. Broke the story that former ambassador Joseph Wilson's trip was arranged by his wife. Novak's column triggered a Justice Department probe that threw the White House into a three-year crisis.

OTTO REICH. Cuban-born anti-Communist and foreign policy expert. President Bush made him a recess appointment as the State Department's top Latin American diplomat.

SENATOR PAT ROBERTS. Republican from Kansas and former Senate Intelligence Committee chairman, his investigations consistently disproved CIA allegations against the Bush administration.

SENATOR JAY ROCKEFELLER. Democrat from West Virginia who used his position on the Senate Intelligence Committee to attack the Bush administration.

KARL ROVE. President Bush's chief political advisor, he was a target in the Valerie Plame investigation.

DONALD RUMSFELD. Former secretary of defense. He worked to make the military more self-sufficient in intelligence collection and terrorist hunting. The CIA viewed Rumsfeld and his staff as rivals.

WILLIAM SCHNEIDER JR. Chairman of the Defense Science Board.

MICHAEL SULICK. A veteran spy in Europe who quit his post in the clandestine service in protest against Porter Goss's staff.

GEORGE TENET. Former CIA director. A Clinton holdover in the Bush administration, he led the CIA when it made enormous blunders before the September 11, 2001, terrorist attacks and in the run-up to the invasion of Iraq in 2003. He went on to write a self-exculpatory book about his experiences.

JOSEPH WILSON. Former ambassador who disclosed a CIA fact-finding trip to Niger in the *New York Times* and then complained when it was revealed that his wife, a clandestine CIA officer, got him the job. Worked for the John Kerry campaign.

VALERIE PLAME WILSON. CIA clandestine officer who got her husband a fact-finding trip to Niger, spawning the Bush administration's worst scandal.

ABU MUSAB AL-ZARQAWI. The leader of al Qaeda in Iraq. Special operations forces and the CIA used innovative technology to find and kill him.

ACKNOWLEDGMENTS

Thanks to Ryan McKibben, Vivienne Sosnowski, Michael Phelps, and Stephen G. Smith of the *Examiner* newspapers for their encouragement and support while I wrote *Sabotage*.

The project could not have been started in 2006 without the backing of my former editors, Wes Pruden, Fran Coombs, and Ken Hanner of the *Washington Times*. *Times* researcher John Sopko helped with fact-checking.

Regnery Publishing's Marji Ross, Harry Crocker, and Paula Currall made the manuscript better.

Not a paragraph was written without the assistance of unnamed current and former intelligence community employees.

APPENDIX

UNPUBLISHED ARTICLE BY COLONEL DAVID HARVEY

Author's Note: In 2005, Colonel Harvey wrote a paper intended for a service publication. Harvey is considered one of the military's leading experts on Iraq and its complex insurgency. He was an Iraq specialist at the Defense Intelligence Agency, then became an advisor to the Joint Chiefs of Staff, ultimately moving with General David Petraeus to Iraq to brief him on the enemy. General Petraeus, then commander of the U.S. Combined Arms Center at Fort Leavenworth, read Harvey's article and told him not to publish it because it was too damning. Below is the article in its entirety.

The insurgency in Iraq that is entwined with the global war on terror is the nation's top national security problem. If it succeeds in frustrating our strategic national security objectives, we will suffer a major defeat in Iraq, the Middle East, and the GWOT [global war on terror] with far-reaching implications affecting not only our immediate security but our influence among the nations of the world. In order to be successful, intelligence is essential to successful counter-insurgency operations in Iraq as well as global counter-terrorism. The key to defeating the insurgency is a deep, intimate, and clinical understanding of the insurgent phenomenon leading to actionable intelligence and effective counter-insurgent programs. Unfortunately, even after more than three years of conflict, we have yet to organize our intelligence assets efficiently and use our intelligence capability to best advantage.

The Iraq insurgency is a complex and adaptive phenomenon. It uses internal and external information operations, sophisticated leveraging of resources (personnel, money, logistics, etc.), and business networks, similar to al Qaeda networks. Yet, even recognizing these capabilities, inadequate efforts to develop the capability to understand the characteristics and specific details of the insurgency and terrorist network we are confronting continues to allow foreign terrorists, hostile state actors, and Iraqi networks outside Iraq to both operate, as well as intermingle with and support, Iraqi insurgents.

The deficiencies in intelligence capability may be summarized as a lack of unified effort and priority. The military effort inside Iraq continues to be neither robust nor cohesive. And the non-military national intelligence community—FBI, Treasury, DIA, and CIA all-source efforts—are not doing enough to identify the networks that are moving foreign fighters/suicide bombers to Iraq, nor have they adequately identified the specific components of the insurgent networks within and external to Iraq, including key nodes, leadership, facilitators, bomb-makers, and financial support systems. In general, resources dedicated to this are insufficient and the architecture to share information and develop finished actionable intelligence are virtually nonexistent. To recover the intelligence initiative, we need to rapidly address intelligence shortcomings and energize efforts to retool, reorient, and resource intelligence for the counter-insurgency in Iraq, or risk losing this conflict with all the adverse consequences to our standing as a nation and our overall national security that such a loss would entail. It is still our war to win, but we cannot succeed without the intelligence capabilities needed to do it while there is still time.

THE PROBLEM: OLD THINK VS. DEMANDS FOR COIN

We begin to perceive the scope and gravity of the problem by first examining the prevailing policy mindset. In the first place, we have not adequately redesigned and resourced our intelligence architecture to shift from early 2003 "major combat operations" structure to an intelligence process and architecture optimized to carry out counter-insurgency operations (COIN). The Iraq COIN problem requires a dedicated architecture significantly more complex and difficult than that established for Operation Iraqi Freedom— one that emphasizes human intelligence over technical. The intelligence challenge surrounding Operation 1003-V was fairly straightforward. However, modest adjustments and incomplete measures and actions over the last three years have neither created the architecture nor provided the resources needed. The more important unresolved issues and challenges are summarized as follows.

Low priority of effort

Unfortunately, Iraq is not the number one priority for the DIA and the CIA, and has not been given priority resources, nor have they been linked fully with other national global counter-terrorism efforts in an effective way. Rather, the counter-insurgency war in Iraq has largely been treated as if it is merely a short-term "contingency" operation that will "work itself out" over time. This stands in stark contrast to the view of the other side. The international terrorist increasingly looks at Iraq as the opportunity for what Clausewitz referred to as a "battlefield" decision. Iraq for our adversaries is the central theater of confrontation with the West and its point of maximum effort, as in evidence by the wide variety of foreign fighter recruits showing up among the insurgent forces. To achieve this decision, the collection of terrorist and insurgent elements both in Iraq and outside constitute a "learning organization" totally dedicated to victory. This is starkly evident in their demonstrated ability to continually and rapidly modify operations and surge

levels of violence in a coordinated manner at key points of time to counter-
act progress in the all-important Iraqi political process. To effectively counter
this effort requires an intelligence structure that is at least as robust, flexible,
rapid, and aggressive as the enemy's, and which benefits from thoroughly
focused application and adequate resources. Currently, the architecture has
not been developed and adequate resources have not been provided.

Efforts to establish such a structure are hampered by the view of some key
policy leaders at the seat of government who continue to assert that the problem of Iraq may be managed in isolation from other global issues or concerns
as a regional issue—and that therefore operational activity associated with
terrorism in Iraq is a CENTCOM and MNF-I [Multi-National Force–Iraq]
issue and must be dealt with by these organizations. Such a view is anachro-
nistic and myopic, rendering a distorted interpretation of the problem
because of artificial distinctions that are not relevant to the current COIN
environment, and run counter to the effort needed to win both the war in
Iraq and the global war over time. Yet while some on our side choose to see
this conflict through the ossified lens of institutional myopia, the international jihadist support network and elements of neighboring governments
make no distinctions with regard to limits artificially imposed by national
borders, nor between the war in Iraq and the war against the U.S. and its allies
in their active support of insurgents. These realities mean that the artificial
distinctions we impose on ourselves by attempting to coordinate and manage the intelligence pieces and operations in pieces via geographic Combatant Commands constrains and impedes the clarity of our understanding with
regard to the key role intelligence plays in mapping the enemy, his centers of
gravity, and key vulnerabilities and developing counter-measures. The consequences are ineffective organizations inadequately resourced, plagued by
dysfunctional processes that do not optimize available resources through syn-

chronization and interagency cooperation. These continue to produce confused, disparate, and often divergent analytical conclusions with equally dysfunctional operational efforts and results.

Lack of a comprehensive system of collection and analysis that integrates both past and current information, identifies priority intelligence gaps, and develops both deep understanding and actionable information

For example, a primary indicator of Coalition deficiencies in intelligence assets and capabilities is starkly evident in the fact that tons of Iraqi Ba'ath Party documents, including intelligence service and terrorist liaison data from the previous regime, remain untranslated and unexploited. It highly is likely that these documents contain a veritable set of Rosetta Stones for understanding the key relationships of the current largely Sunni-driven insurgency.

Failure to exploit available technology and to match manpower resources to technology

The Department of Defense and the intelligence community wrongfully regard technical solutions to intelligence collection as a panacea. That said, the enormous advantages the U.S. could enjoy because of its overwhelming technical capabilities are largely underutilized, while the intelligence community continues to use outmoded and inefficient technology such as disparate service or ineffective joint Operation Iraqi Freedom war-fighting databases, marginal software applications, bad data management, and lack of access to basic systems. In addition, there is currently no holistic COIN methodology or approach that matches manpower requirements to technology and industry tools and methods already in existence.

Lack of joint, integrated, interagency effort for the analysis and production needed to identify, track, and attack international networks and the people in them

A fully integrated analytical process would result in greatly enhanced and broader situational understanding and meaningful comprehensive intelligence for use at all levels: tactical, operational, and strategic. Such an effort, multi-tiered and decentralized in the forward AOR [area of responsibility]— yet centrally coordinated in Washington—for continuous comprehensive analysis over time requires the following ingredients currently missing:

- ☐ Investigative work similar to police dealing with gangs/mafia
- ☐ Network, relationship, cultural, pattern, and financial analysis
- ☐ Cultural and anthropological knowledge to include religious, ethnic, social, political, and economic, and exceptional ability to understand people, culture, and motivations
- ☐ Knowledge of Saddam-era professional, security, party organizations, roles, and missions
- ☐ Continuity on the problem—the status quo of rotating analysts undermines the development of the depth of expertise required to be successful. This rapid rotation of analysts is driven by the practice of treating Iraq as a contingency operation like Bosnia: a problem to be managed, not a war to be won.
- ☐ Stabilization of analysts working Iraq—in effect a stop-loss

Lack of a "center of excellence"

Currently, we do not currently have a national level "center of excellence" that provides specific operational and strategic analytical focus on the insurgency leadership, organization, financing, and tactics (including IEDs), as well as comprehensive mapping of networked relations to global terrorist organizations. As a result, we do not have an effective, comprehensive, and integrated "map" with which to dissect the insurgency. What we do have are a number of disparate, narrowly focused, and marginally resourced elements struggling to satisfy a range of different bosses with high-level demands that focus on immediate situation awareness and the news of the day. Moreover, the plethora of existing organizations continue to needlessly duplicate each other's efforts, spending time and manpower building what is uniformly the same general current intelligence picture, but short on intelligence specifics that are most needed. In addition, there is overemphasis on answering current intelligence questions and developing data points to counter activity generated by CNN-type headline news. This reactionary process consumes time and resources that starves and undermines the effort to collect information and provide a detailed analysis and mapping of the insurgency.

Personnel and organizational turbulence

MNF-I and Corps analytical efforts are seriously hindered by rotations in theater and lack of experienced analysts with limited expertise, compounded by significant operational demands and legacy analysis and data management issues. Additionally, Divisions and below are overtasked, with their focus on the current fight and force protection. The lack of an overarching supporting architecture to provide both a common intelligence picture as well as greater focused detail that maps links between insurgents, terrorists, and their supporters means that no one is providing the integration and comprehensive analysis across division boundaries—much less unified command or national boundaries—to provide the vitally needed complete picture of the insurgency to include pinpointing leaders and leadership relationships, financing, IED networks, and links between Sunni Arab extremists, former regime loyalists, and Sunni Arab society.

Focused, well-resourced analytical efforts needed to effectively
understand and target enemy forces

To identify and destroy/neutralize the insurgent and terrorist infrastruc-
tures and systems that support them, their organizations and relationships
must be targeted completely. To achieve our goals, we need to attack the key
processes that sustain the insurgency—leadership, recruitment, logistics,
resource gathering, finances, communications, movement, documentation,
access, ideological support, and IO. The current capability to provide such
a picture on anything near the scale required does not exist.

THE SOLUTION: SIX STEPS TO SIGNIFICANT IMPROVEMENT

Create a dedicated national-level joint interagency "center of
excellence" to provide both a deployable as well as reach back
for integrated tactical, operational, and strategic-level analysis
of the insurgency

A "center of excellence" organization would provide to the National Command Authority, Unified Commanders, and Joint commander in the field a
means to establish priorities, coordinate production, and exploit all means
to get a detailed identification of insurgency leadership, organization, financing, weapons, and support networks. To be maximally effective, this entity
must work for the White House or the director of the National Security
Council because the center must have the ability to access political authority
at a very high level for decision and approved action in order to effectively
respond to opportunities, breaking developments, and unanticipated problems as they arise in prosecuting the war. Such a center would comprehen-
sively map, analyze, and synthesize information to dissect the insurgency
inside and outside Iraq. It would provide to the National Command authority a complete picture of not only regional insurgencies, but also the global
links between them, thus providing a means of assessing organizational struc-

ture, intent, and evolution over time, and furnish informed recommendations to decision-makers.

The center of excellence would have the authority to levy tiered requirements on each joint and interagency organization within their capabilities to share and transfer past, current, and new information and intelligence—for analysis to then be placed in context by the center.

Currently, joint organizations (IC, COCOMs, and MNF-I) receive no integrated guidance with which to deconflict intelligence production. Instead, they use their limited intelligence resources duplicating and creating their own version of the current intelligence picture, while detailed and required term intelligence is not done. Such a linkage between the center and deployed personnel would provide an enormous boost in the quality of support to the overall tactical effort by providing a more complete common picture of the insurgency leadership, financing, IED networks, and links between extremists, former regime elements, and Sunni Arab society. To establish this center we should do the following:

☐ Hire 200 analysts (not all intelligence) permanently assigned to a Joint Inter-Agency Task Force (JIATF) with the background, experience, and specialties to exploit data.

☐ Require at least a one-star general or SES leadership.

☐ Use J-2 Office of Iraq Analysis (OIA) (currently more than seventy people) as the core of the new JIATF. Identify the top fifty experienced analysts who have served in Iraq and assign them to OIA. The DIA would provide an additional forty people, and the NSA, the NGA [National Geospatial-Intelligence Agency], and the CIA provide the balance.

☐ Rotate members of team to Iraq to insure support/access to data.

☐ Require interagency participation to include integration of IED and financial task force intelligence with Iraq-focused terrorist analysis.

☐ Ensure full transparency between Iraq insurgency analysis and analysis on Syria and Iran (especially the activities of the Iranian Revolutionary Guard Corps and Qods Force). Important elements of these nation state governments are intent on making war against the U.S. in Iraq. Any boundary between Iraq COIN analysis and Syria/Iraq country analysis is artificial.

☐ Establish use of relational database for mapping/tracking and co-locate information dominance database with the task force.

☐ Eliminate artificial boundaries and divisions between analytical efforts regarding Iraq.

☐ Develop relationships with appropriate defense contractors and academic institutions to exploit advanced tools, methods, approaches, and knowledge.

Change policy to stabilize personnel and expertise

The analytical efforts of the MNF-I and the Corps are greatly hindered by the constant rotation of skilled personnel in and out of theater, which means a lack of continuity in the support from experienced analysts. Moreover, when intelligence personnel are in theater, they are usually focused on operational/tactical demands, do not have a methodology to develop and sustain an integrated complete picture across division boundaries, and use substandard legacy systems and data management tools. A cadre of stabilized in-theater intelligence personnel should funnel data to the center of excellence for the multifaceted, detailed, cross-boundary, and complex analytical work required to penetrate and destroy the insurgency.

Change personnel rules to emphasize recruiting / permit "cherry-picking" the best and the brightest for the intelligence effort

Personnel recruiting policy should establish a priority on finding, recruiting, and dedicating personnel who demonstrate skill and desire for this difficult work—and assign these analysts to the mission until the job is done. Such a personnel policy would develop special rules for rotating experienced Iraqi and functional analysts among the various analytical levels/organizations (tactical, operational, and strategic).

Fix DOCEX [document exploitation system]

Make this system a priority supported with translators, analytical support, and additional contractor focus to exploit captured documents focused on Iraqi intelligence archives, presidential archives, and the ministries of foreign affairs, trade, and defense to inform us about the current insurgency and trans-regional terrorist ties. To do this, we need to:

- ☐ Organize more effectively so documents are translated, tagged, organized topically, searchable, and easily retrievable
- ☐ Exploit huge volume of captured Saddam-era documents to shed light on pre–Operation Iraqi Freedom regime activities, practices, and capabilities. This work can be performed anywhere, and because the documents are "legacy materials," they can be translated by native speakers with low or no clearance. The only requirement is that the translation be accurate. Actual analysis of translated materials can be carried out by analysts with appropriate clearances.

Exploit DOCEX for links to trans-regional terrorists

Accelerate efforts to get un-processed documents into the database, with focus on trans-regional terror ties.

Improve interrogation productivity

We still have insufficient interrogators and translators, but increased and focused analytical support and prioritization would significantly improve the production of meaningful information. We need to link this effort with Step 1 above, while developing the approach to migrate the knowledge and skills of the U.S. organization to the Iraqis.

LETTER FROM CONGRESSMAN PETE HOEKSTRA
TO PRESIDENT GEORGE W. BUSH

Congressman Pete Hoekstra, then chairman of the House Intelligence Committee, wrote to President Bush about a number of CIA issues. Paramount was the congressman's belief that elements within Langley headquarters were working to undermine the White House.

U.S. HOUSE OF REPRESENTATIVES
PERMANENT SELECT COMMITTEE ON INTELLIGENCE

May 18, 2006

The Honorable George W. Bush
President
The White House
Washington, D.C. 20500

Dear Mr. President:

I write to address three issues of great importance to me, and, for that matter, to our collective efforts to improve intelligence. I wish to address the nominees for leading the CIA, very briefly discuss concerns about intelligence reform in general, and, finally, the oversight of intelligence activities of the U.S. Government.

First, I am concerned that the nominations for Director and Deputy Director of the Central Intelligence Agency signal a retreat from needed reforms of the Agency. I have respectfully shared my strong concerns regarding these nominees, and I think it would be an understatement to say that I am disappointed that Congress was never consulted on either of these choices. I have clearly stated my objections for the Director's position based on what I perceive to be a very real need to have a civilian lead this fundamentally and essentially civilian organization. My position here is purely principled and substantive. However, the choice for Deputy Director, Steve Kappes, is more troubling, both on a substantive and personal level. Allow me to explain.

I have taken great pride in the work that we have been able to accomplish, together with the Adminintzation, to reform, improve, and empower our intelligence capabilities to protect the Nation. Regrettably, the appointment of Mr. Kappes sends a clear signal that the days of collaborative reform between the White House and this committee may be over. I am concerned that the strong objections - not just about this personnel selection - are being dismissed completely, pezhaps sending us back to a past, less cooperative relattionship, at a time when so much more needs to be done. Individuals both within and outside the Administration have let me and others know of their strong opposition to this choice for Deputy Director. Yet, in my conversations with General Hayden it is clear that the decision on Mr. Kappes is final. Collaboration is what got us successful intelligence reform. Why would we want to eschew such a relationzhip and process that proved so successful? Unfortunately, it is beginning to appear that we have evolved, on several levels, to a different philosophical direction for intelligence reform. I'm disappointed by this because there was such hope for progress after

9/11 and the successful passage of the reform bill in December of 2004.

I understand that Mr. Kappes is a capable, well-qualified, and well-liked former Directorate of Operations (DO) case officer. I am heartened by the professional qualities he would bring to the job, but am concerned by what could be the political problems that he could bring back to the agency. There has been much public and private speculation about the politicization of the Agency. I am convinced that this politicization was underway well before Porter Goss became the Director. In fact, I have been long concerned that a strong and well-positioned group within the Agency intentionally undermined the Administration and its policies. This argument is supported by the Ambassador Wilson/Valerie Plame events, as well as by the string of unauthorized disclosures from an organization that prides itself with being able to keep secrets. I have come to the belief that, despite his service to the DO, Mr. Kappes may have been part of this group. I must take note when my Democratic colleagues - those who so vehemently denounced and publicly attacked the strong choice of Porter Goss as Director - now publicly support Mr. Kappes's return.

Further, the details surrounding Mr. Kappes's departure from the CIA give me great pause. Mr. Kappes was not fired, but, as I understand it, summarily resigned his position shortly after Director Goss responded to his demonstrated contempt for Congress and the Intelligence Committees' oversight responsibilities. The fact is, Mr. Kappes and his Deputy, Mr. Sulick, were developing a communications offensive to bypass the Intelligence Committees and the CIA's own Office of Congressional Affairs. One can only speculate on the motives but it clearly indicates a willingness to promote a personal agenda. Every day we suffer from the consequences of individuals promoting their personal agendas. This is clearly a place at which we do not want or need to be.

Second, I am concerned that the Administration is not implementing the carefully defined role of the DNI we worked so hard to craft. I have publicly expressed my vision, consistent with the intent of the Intelligence Reform and Terrorism Prevention Act of 2004. My view for the Office of the Director of National Intelligence was, and remains, one of a lean, coordinating function that provides "corporate" leadership to the individually high-fidelity intelligence agencies - "corporate divisions" if you will. This vision does not include the DNI "doing" things so much as the DNI "making sure things get done" by the agencies. I am concerned that the current implementation is creating a large, bureaucratic, and hierarchical structure that will be les flexible and agile than our adversaries. I am convinced that if we are to be successful we must limit the growth of the office of the DNI - to force it to be the lean coordinating function we envisioned. Our Fiscal Year 2007 authorization bill fences a number of the new positions at the DNI because of the concerns about this growing bureaucracy. America needs an agile, effective Intelligence Community. I simply wanted you to know that the authorization bill tries to send that clear signal within the context of the growing concern about the implementation of intelligence reform.

Finally, Mr. President, but perhaps most importantly, I want to reemphasize that the Administration has the legal responsibility to "fully and currently" inform the House and Senate Intelligence Committees of its intelligence and intelligence-related activities. Although the law gives you and the committees flexibility on how we accomplish that (I have been fully supportive of your concerns in that respect), it is clear that we, the Congress, are to be provided all information about such activities. I have learned of some alleged Intelligence Community activities about which our committee has not been briefed. In the next few days I will be formally requesting information on these activities. If these allegations are true, they may represent a breach of responsibility by the Administration, a violation of law, and, just as importantly, a direct affront to me and the Members of this committee who have so ardently supported efforts to collect information on our enemies. I strongly encourage you to direct all elements of the Intelligence Community to fulfill their legal responsibility to keep the Intelligence Committees fully briefed on their activities. The U.S. Congress simply should not have to play 'Twenty Questions' to get the information that it deserves under our Constitution.

I've shared these thoughts with the Speaker, and he concurs with my concerns. Regrettably, there are other issues that need to be discussed. What I've provided here are the most pressing. Thank you for your consideration of these items.

    Sincerely yours,

    Pete

Cc: Steve Hadley
Josh Bolton
John Negroponte

QUESTIONNAIRE SENT TO THE CIA
FROM THE JUSTICE DEPARTMENT

This is the questionnaire the Justice Department asks the CIA to fill out after the Agency sends Justice a criminal referral. In the case of Valerie Plame, some in Justice were not impressed by the answer to question number eleven.

QUESTIONS FOR LEAK INVESTIGATIONS

1. Date and identity of the article containing the classified information.

2. Specific statements in the article which are classified and whether the information was properly classified.

3. Whether the classified information disclosed is accurate.

4. Whether the information came from a specific document and, if so, the origin of the document and the name of the individual responsible for the security of the classified data disclosed.

5. The extent of official dissemination of the information.

6. Whether the information has been the subject of prior official release.

7. Whether prior clearance for publication or release of the information was sought from proper authorities.

8. Whether the material or portions thereof or enough background data has been published officially or in the press to make an educated speculation on the matter possible.

9. Whether the information can be made available for use in a prosecution and, if so, the name of the person competent to testify concerning its classification.

10. Whether declassification had been considered or decided upon prior to the publication of the data.

11. What effect the disclosure of the classified information could have on national defense.

LETTER FROM DOUGLAS FEITH TO THE SECURITY APPEALS BOARD ON BEHALF OF MICHAEL MALOOF

THE UNDER SECRETARY OF DEFENSE
2000 DEFENSE PENTAGON
WASHINGTON, DC 20301-2000

POLICY

16 October 2002

MEMORANDUM FOR THE CHAIRMAN
                SECURITY APPEALS BOARD

FROM: Douglas J. Feith, Under Secretary of Defense for Policy ᴬᴶᴰ 10/16/02

SUBJECT: Security Appeals Board Case Concerning Michael Maloof

As you are aware, Michael Maloof is a member of the Policy staff reporting to me directly. I want the Security Appeals Board to know of my confidence in Michael, rooted in his many contributions to national security, his patriotism and sense of duty and his commitment to security.

As Michael's employer, I was briefed on his case. Despite what was outlined in the Statement of Reasons, I do not think Michael's clearances should be removed. I recognize that technical questions have been raised about whether he reported appropriately to the proper office, that is no reason, in my view, to revoke his clearances. His intention to report was clear and he was consistent in filing reports on his foreign contacts and travel experiences relating to his Policy responsibilities. I am confident that if he had experienced any attempt to coerce or manipulate him for information, he would have taken appropriate action and reported that development immediately.

As I understand the record, his relationship with a female Georgian foreign national while he was married was proper and he kept it that way until after he and his wife had separated due to unrelated issues. Sometime after his separation, he reported that he would be entering into a relationship with the Georgian foreign national, whom he has since married. Having known Michael for many years personally and professionally, I do not believe he would have allowed himself to be compromised in any way. On the issue of his personal affairs, including financial issues, he has undertaken a serious, documented effort to straighten them out.

I am proud to have Michael on our team and strongly urge the Security Appeals Board to reinstate all of his clearances to permit him to continue his important work to contribute to our national security.

MICHAEL MALOOF'S 2004 MEMO
CONCERNING INTELLIGENCE GATHERING

19 May 2004

MEMORANDUM FOR THE RECORD

On 02 May 2004 at 1000, I met with Under Secretary of Defense for Policy Doug Feith and his chief of staff, Michael Mobbs, at my request. The meeting took place at the USDP's residence. My intention to meet was to discuss my future course at DOD. Mr. Mobbs also asked me to bring along materials I had in my possession that would be responsive to a series of questions posed by the Senate Intelligence Committee stemming from my prior closed-door session with Staff.

In going through the materials, Mr. Feith looked them over and began to ask me questions concerning information I had obtained from various sources that may have been incorporated in the material I brought. He specifically inquired about my meeting with a representative of the Iraqi National Congress, and the apparent reference to a request that I had made to Richard Perle to pass along to Mr. Ahmed Chalabi, head of the INC. I assured Mr. Feith that the information I gleaned was to help us determine where in the classified domain similar reporting existed.

I then told Mr. Feith of my efforts to bring information to the attention of the authorities based on what human sources have provided to me. I proceeded to show him some of my recent memos to his former military assistant, Col. Kathleen Pivarsky. More recent information reflected

- Information of upcoming terrorist attacks being planned in Lebanon against U.S. forces in Iraq. Timeframe was in mid to late December 2003 in which I sought to bring it to the attention of officials but the officials refused to follow up on it. Two weeks following my efforts, a series of carbomb attacks commenced in Iraq.
- Very recent inquiry from an influential Mullah offering to assist in the release of U.S. hostages and with our efforts to halt the Iranian nuclear program.
- Syrians had come back a month earlier seeking to set up a discreet backchannel with high level DOD officials.

I advised Mr. Feith of these developments, prompting him to insist that I cease acquiring such information and attempting to pass it through his office or to intelligence circles. He added that I should provide only the name of the contact and a phone number and allow the intelligence community to follow up, if they chose to do so.

I advised Mr. Feith that I had tried that approach as well but there never was any follow up by the intelligence community with the sourcing I had provided. I also pointed out that much of this information was highly perishable and time sensitive. Mr. Feith retorted that this was not my problem. I then asked even if I should stop my attempts even if itt meant losing American lives?, to which Mr. Feith responded, so be it. Mr. Feith expressed growing irritation that I was undertaking this effort and stated that it was all he could do to stop the public perception that I was setting up his office to give the appearance of running a rogue intelligence operation to bypass the intelligence community. He added that he had to deal with the Carl Levins on the Hill who have made such accusations. I further informed Mr. Feith that a lawyer who had met with my source also attempted to reach Mr. Cambone's office and was rudely informed that the information was not wanted. Consequently, the nature of the infomration never was passed.

Mr. Feith made clear that he wanted my attempts to pass information to cease immediately and said that while I was on administrative leave, I technically still worked for him and that he was orderiing me to stop acquiring and ipassing any further information either through his office or to the intelligence community. Mr. Feith said he would send me a letter to that effect. At this writing, I have received no such letter. However, Mr. Mobbs can attest to the facts relating to this exchange.

Michael Maloof
19 May 2004

INDEX